Real World

Colouring Book

For Advanced Users & Adults

50 Images

Created From Real Life Photos
For You To Colour As You Please.

ISBN 978-0-359-86318-1

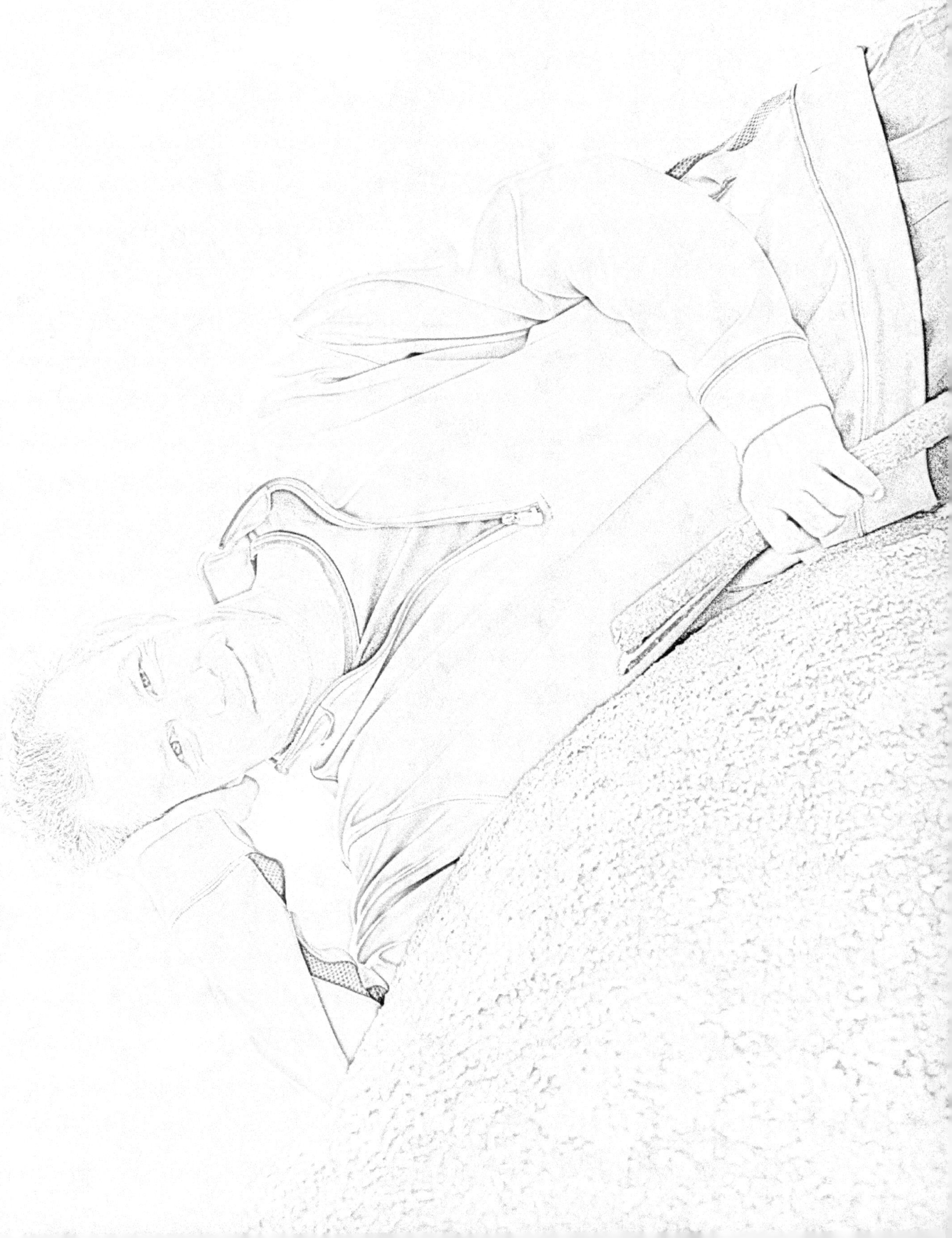

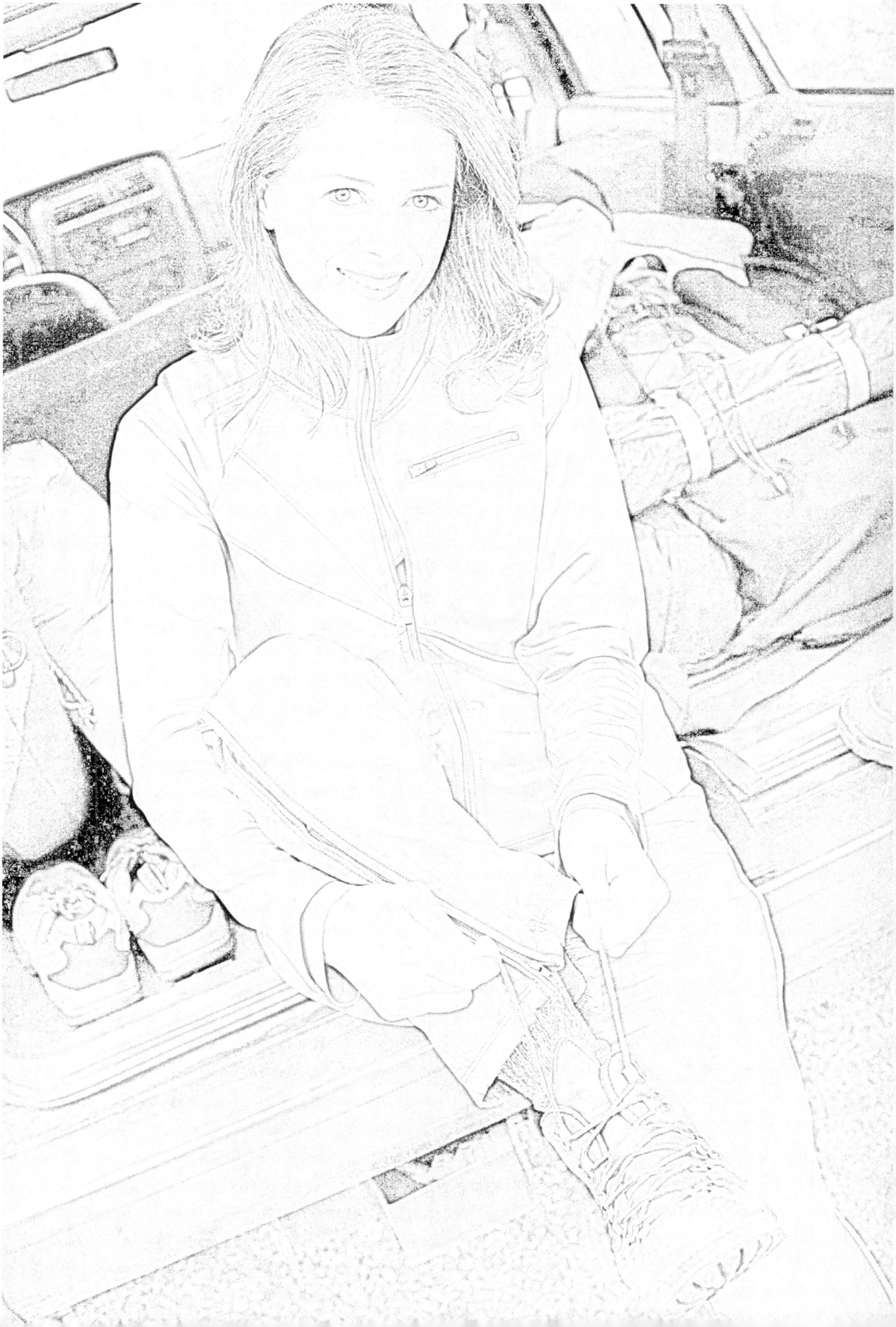

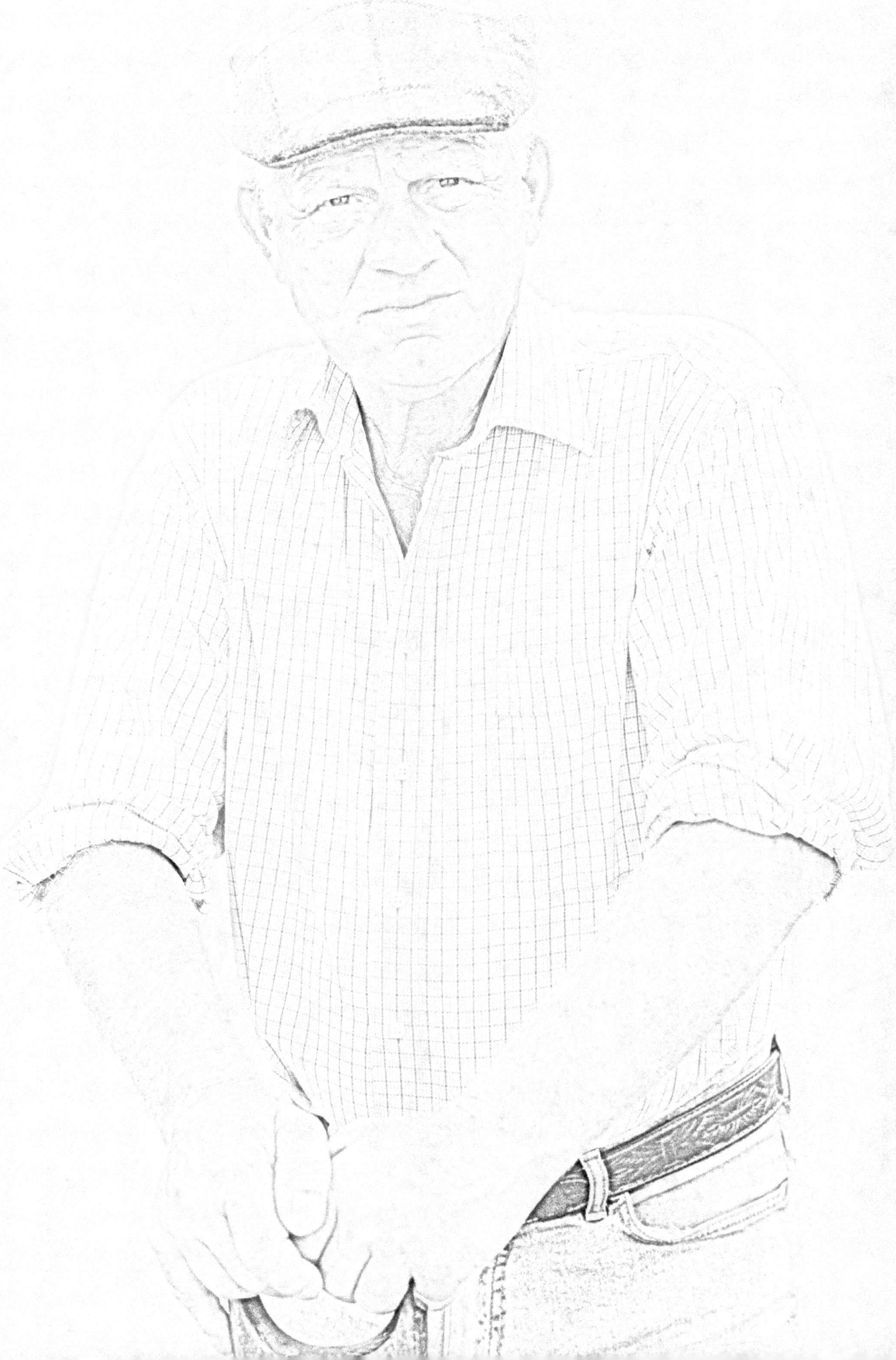

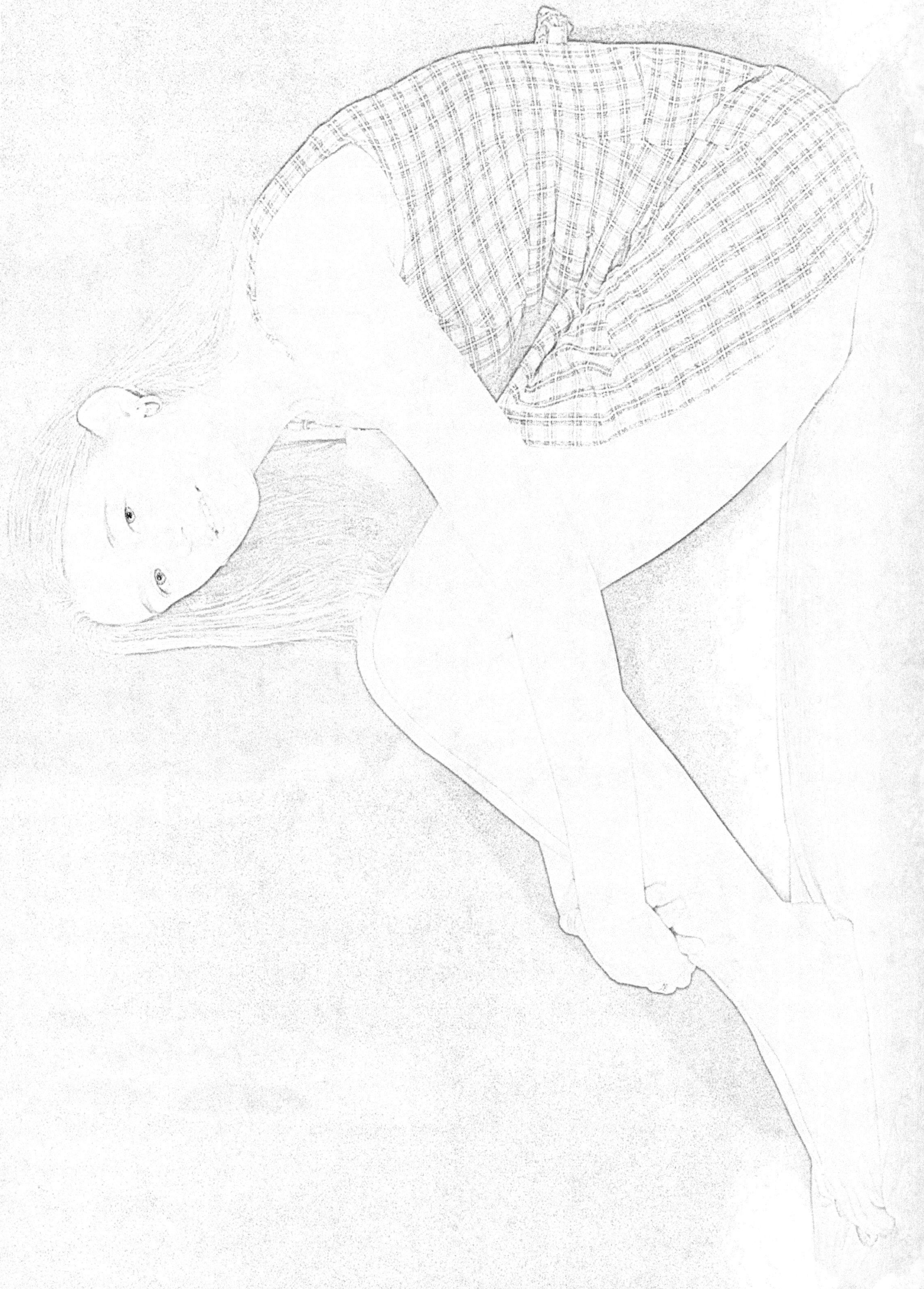

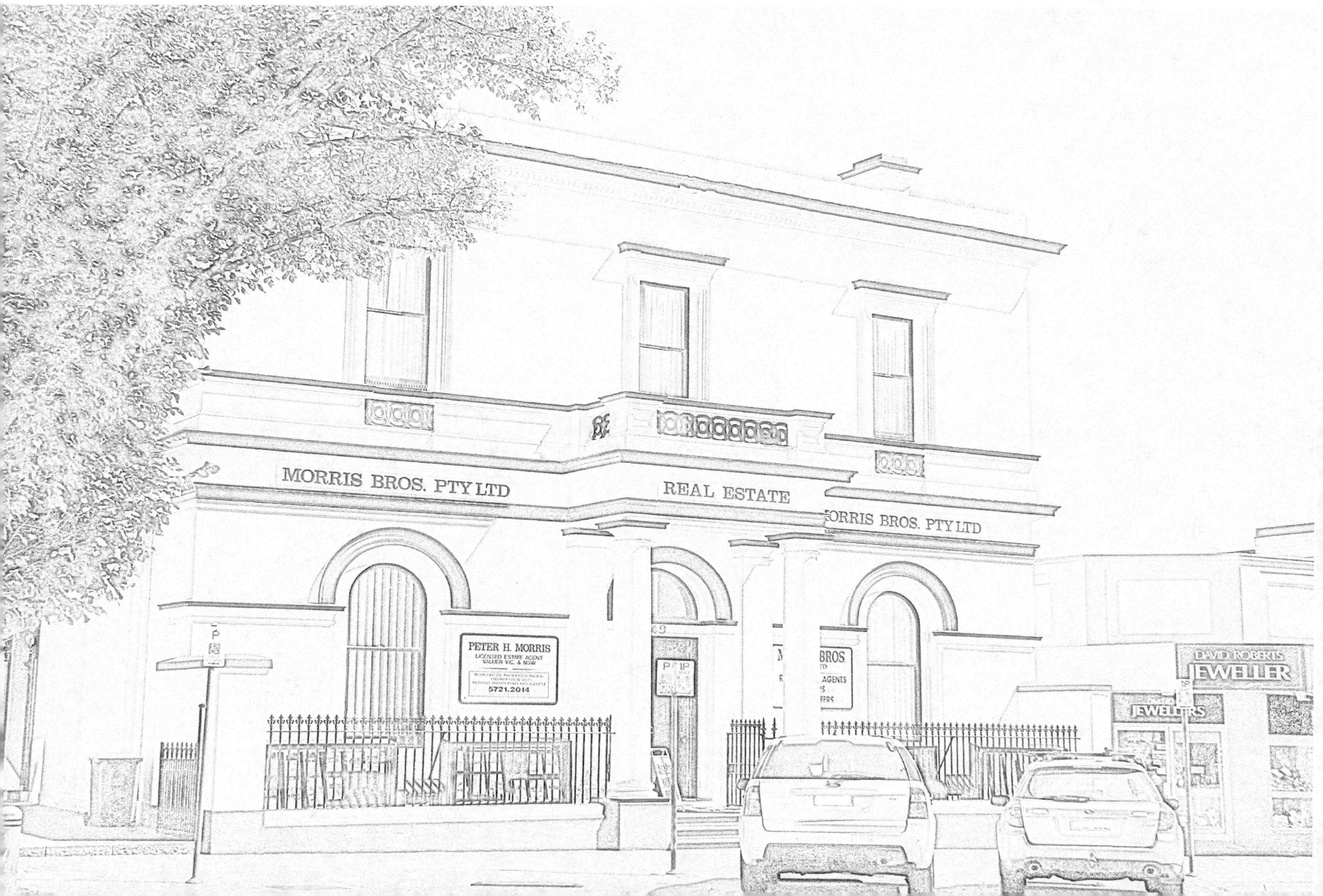

MORRIS BROS. PTY LTD
REAL ESTATE
ORRIS BROS. PTY LTD
PETER H. MORRIS
LICENSED ESTATE AGENT
VALUER VIC. & NSW
5721.2014
DAVID ROBERTS
JEWELLER
JEWELLERS

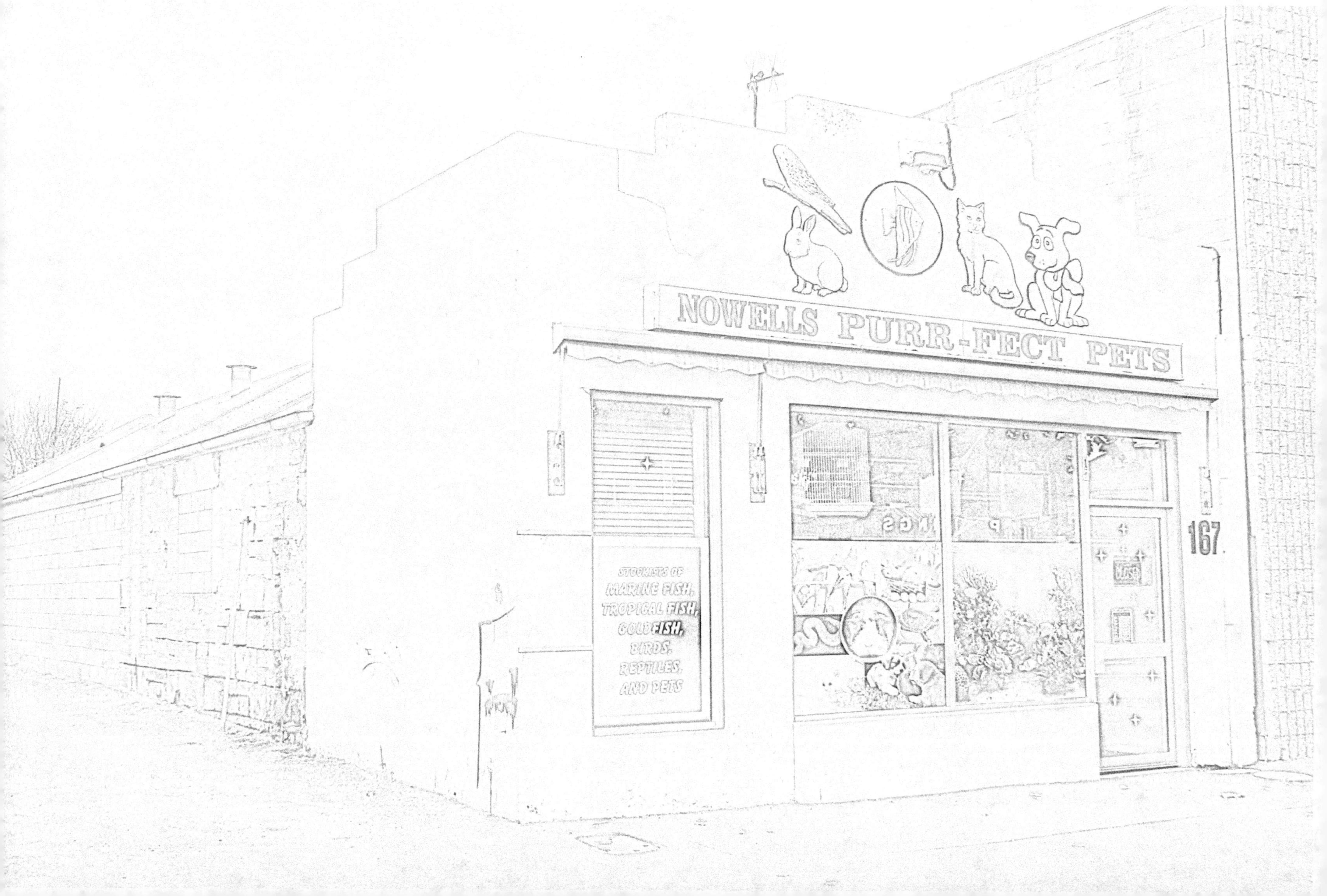
NOWELLS PURR-FECT PETS
167
STOCKISTS OF
MARINE FISH,
TROPICAL FISH,
GOLDFISH,
BIRDS,
REPTILES,
AND PETS

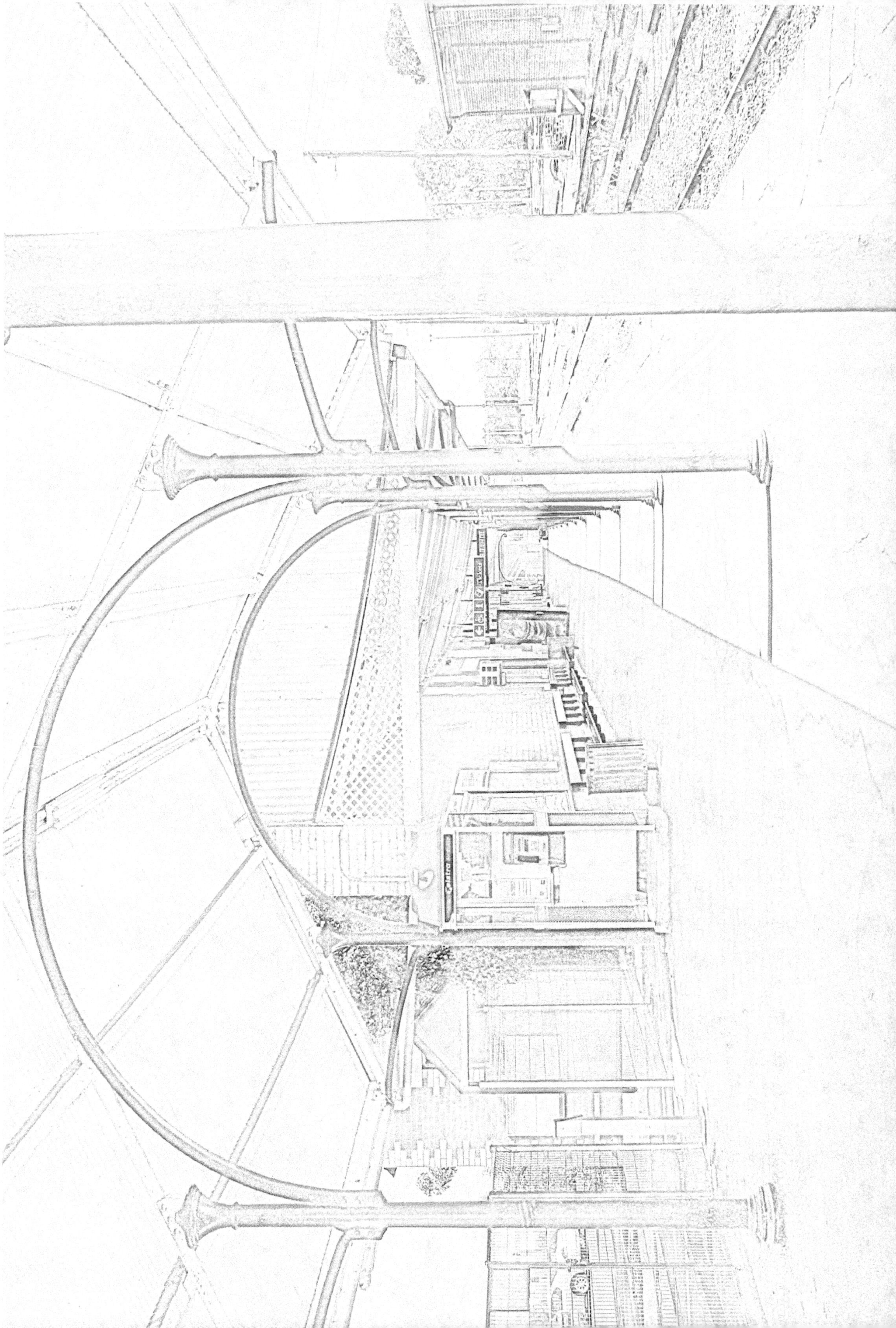

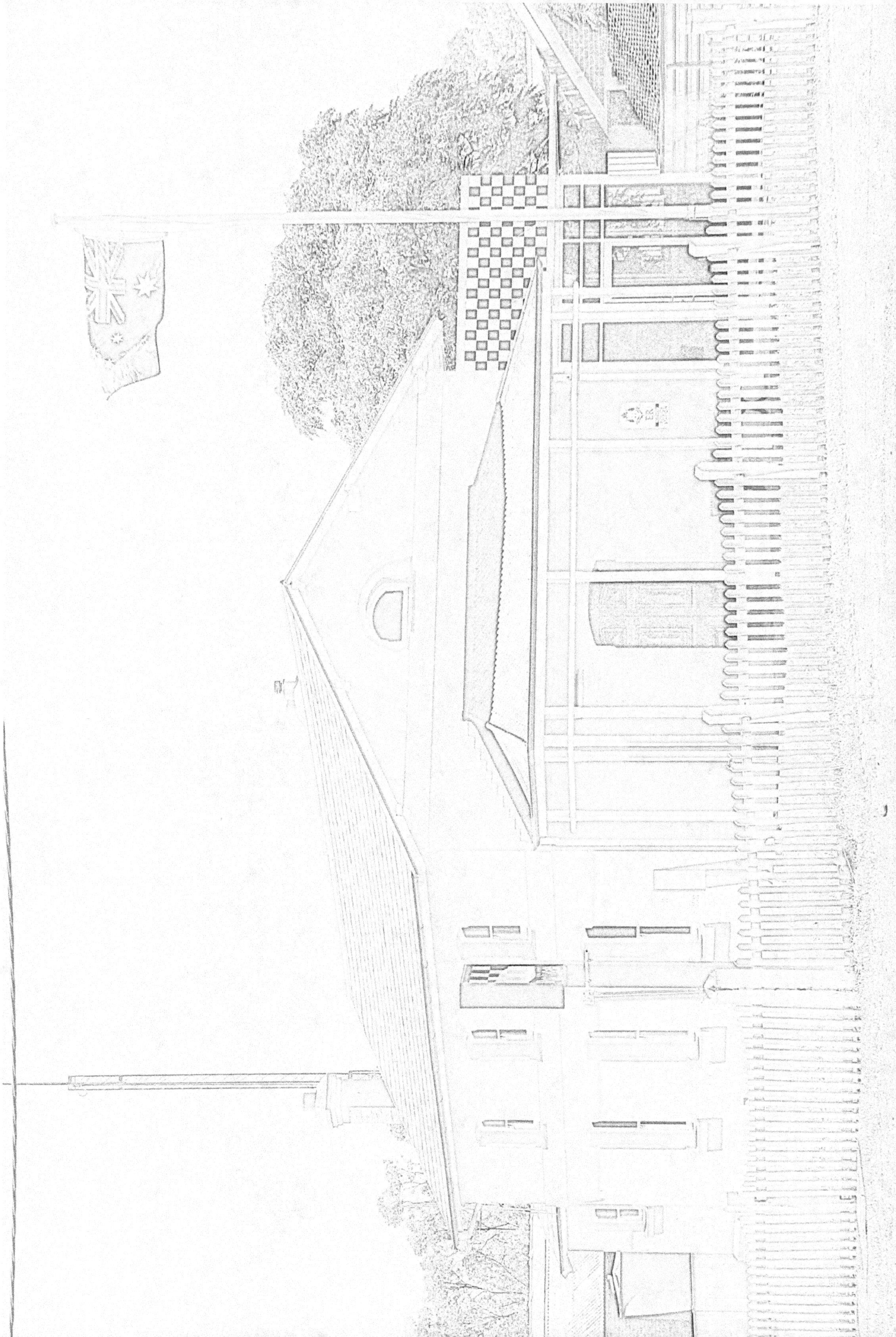

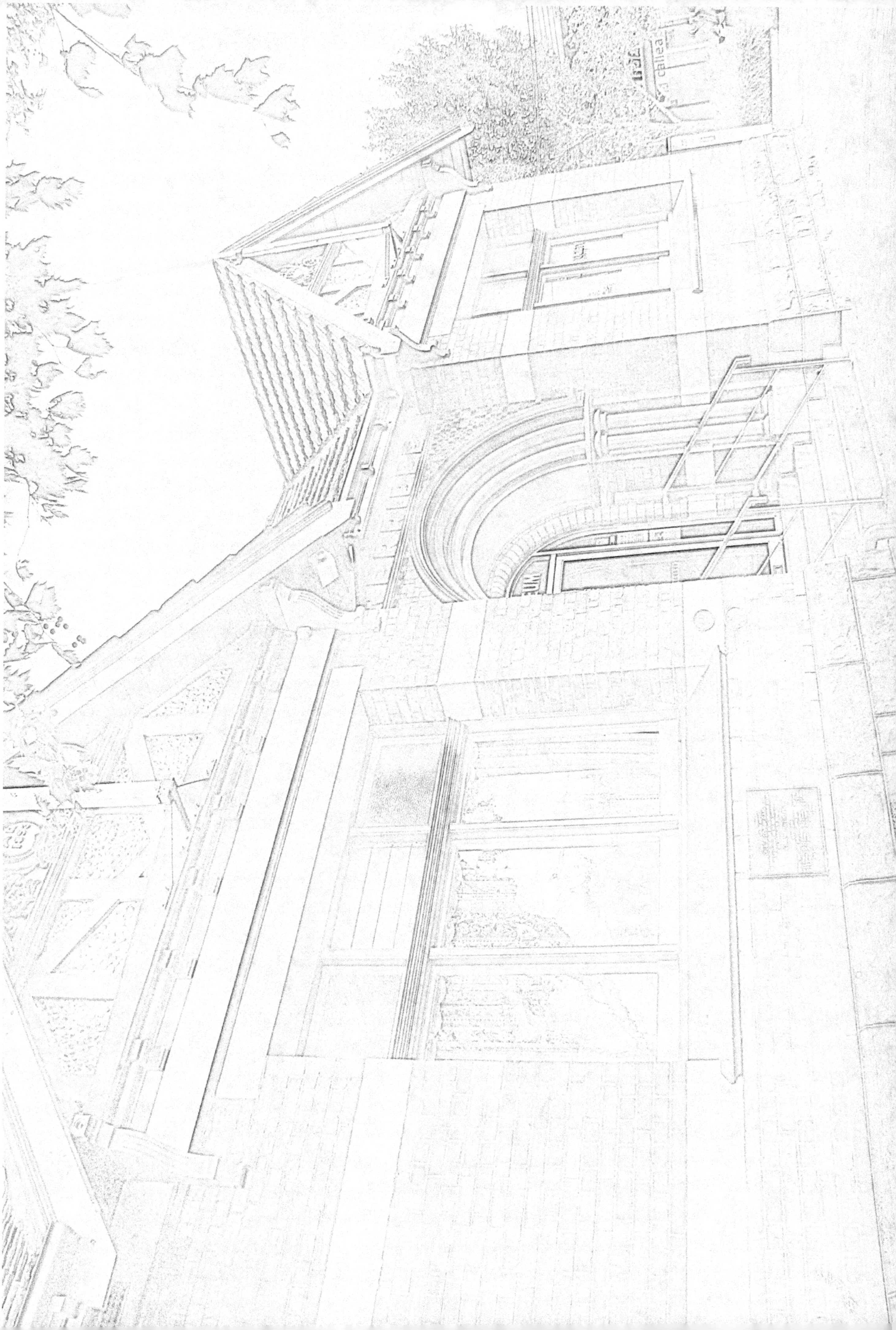

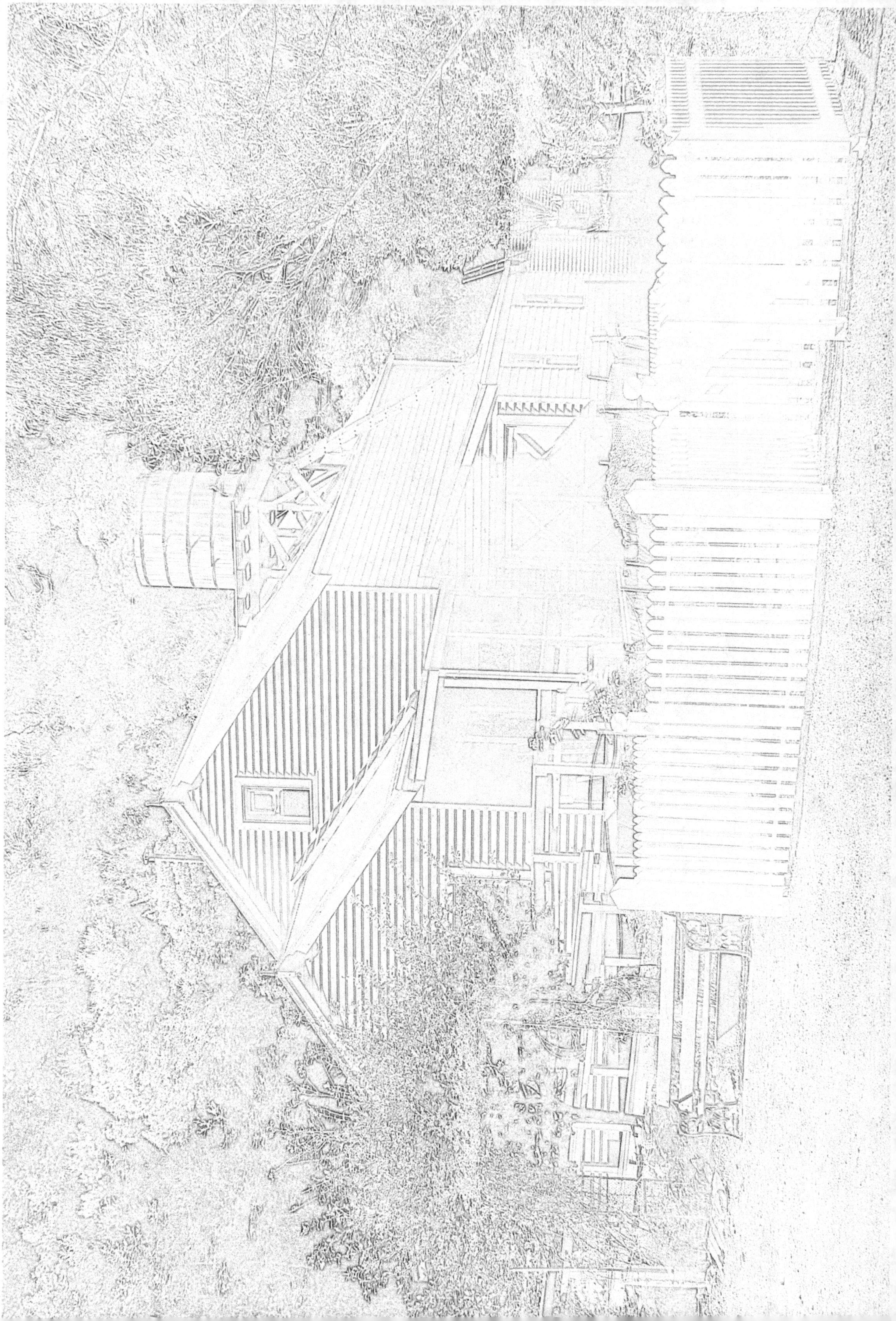

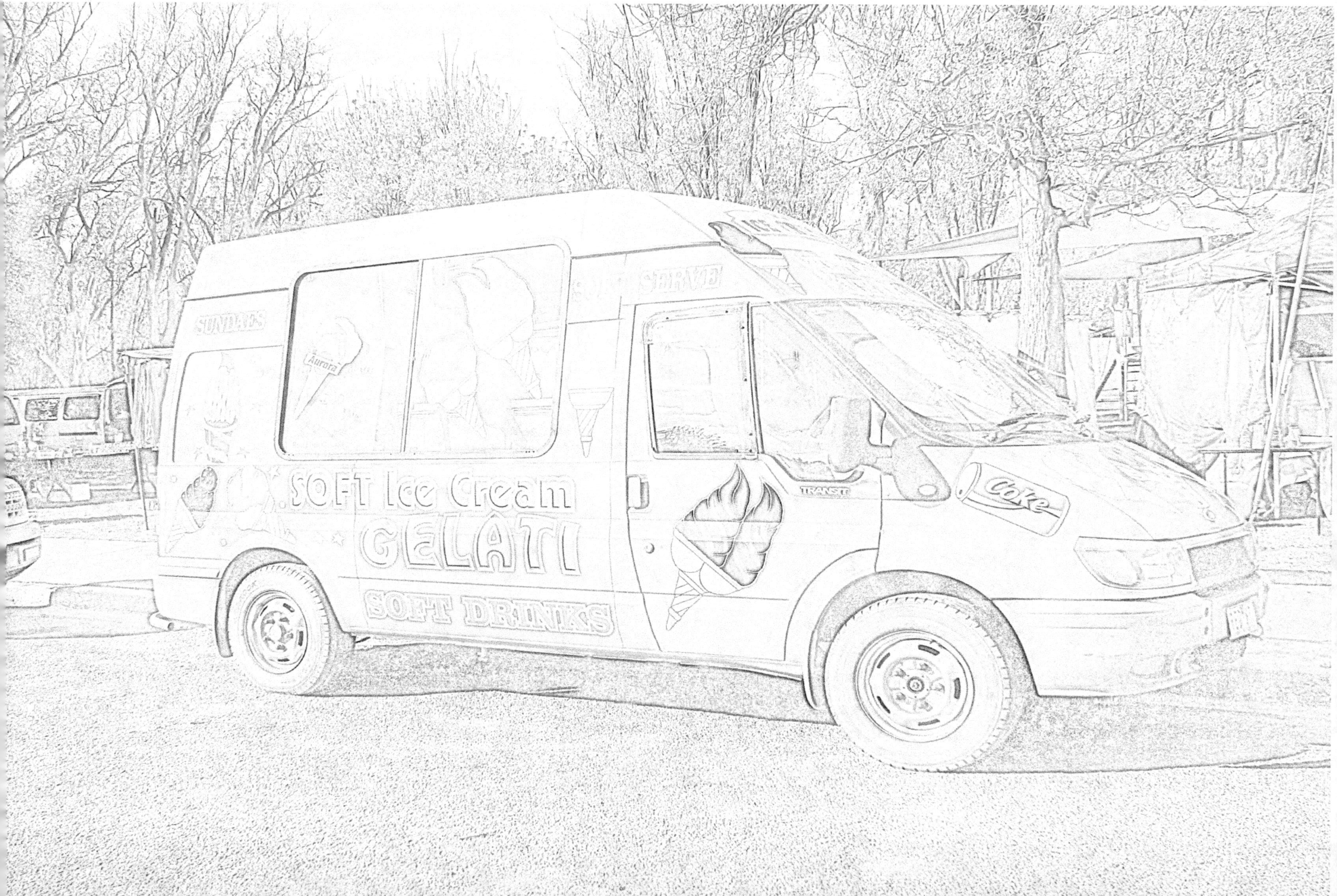
SUNDAES
Aurora
SOFT Ice Cream
GELATI
SOFT DRINKS
TRANSIT
Coke

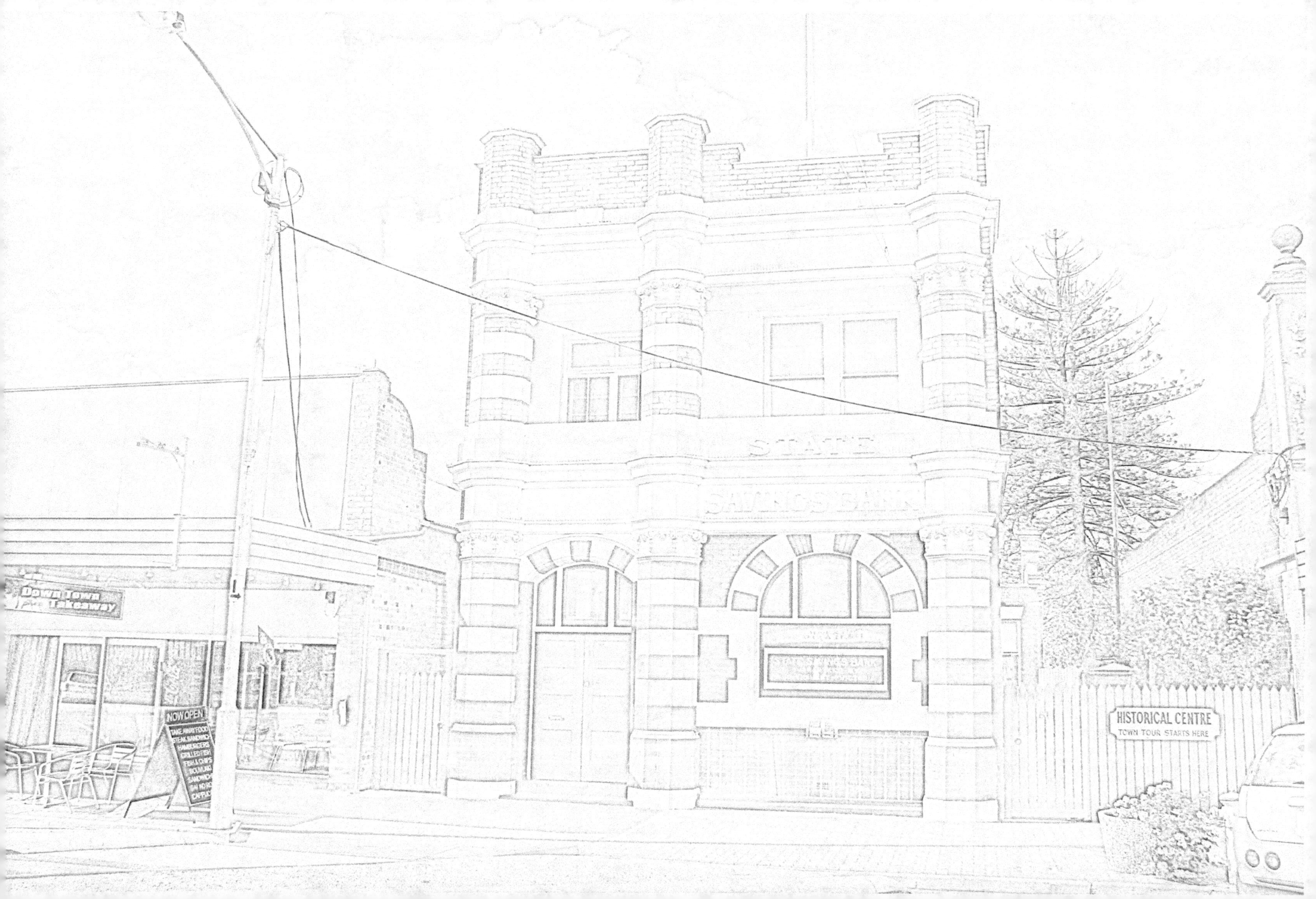
STATE
Down Town
Takeaway
NOW OPEN
HISTORICAL CENTRE
TOWN TOUR STARTS HERE

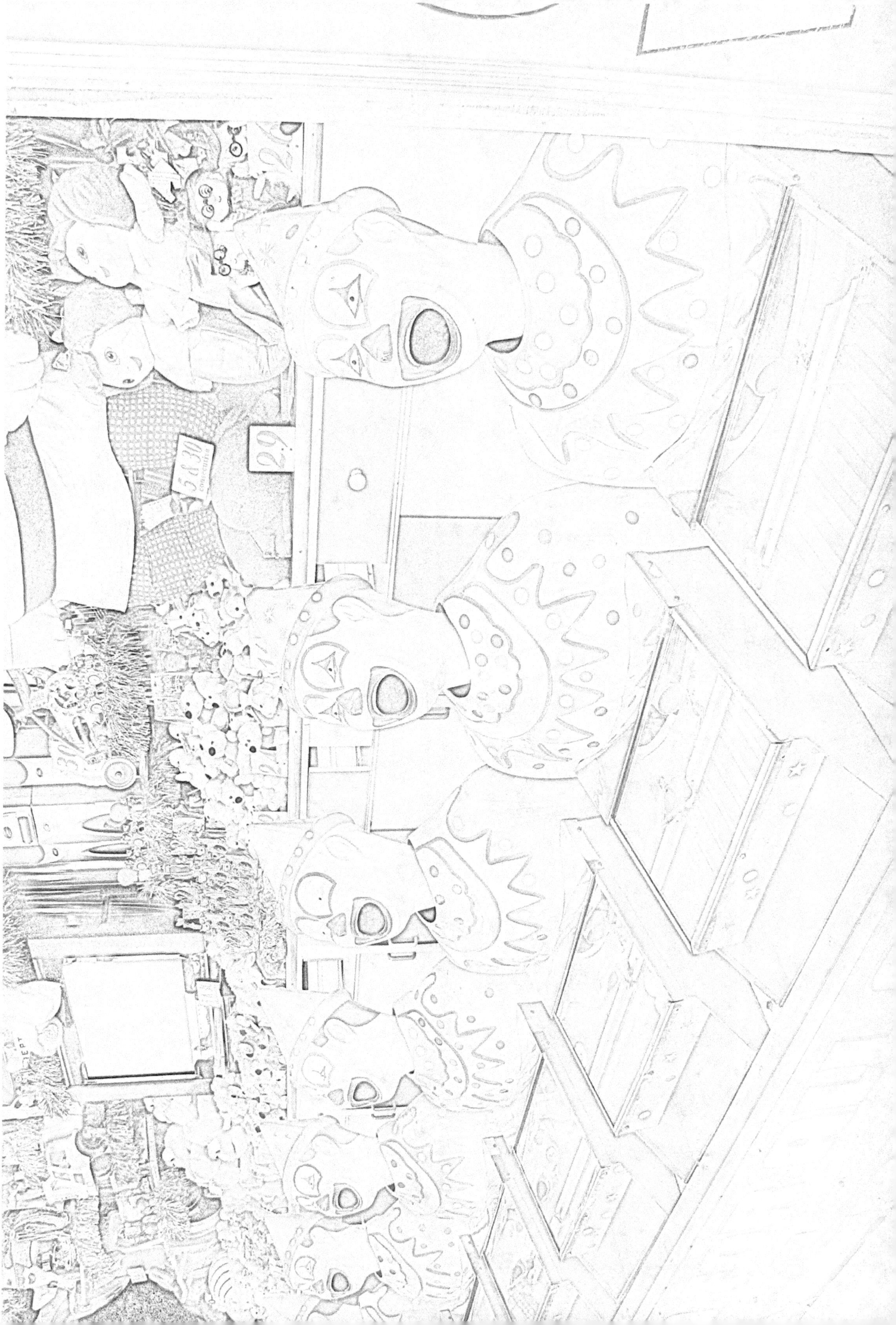

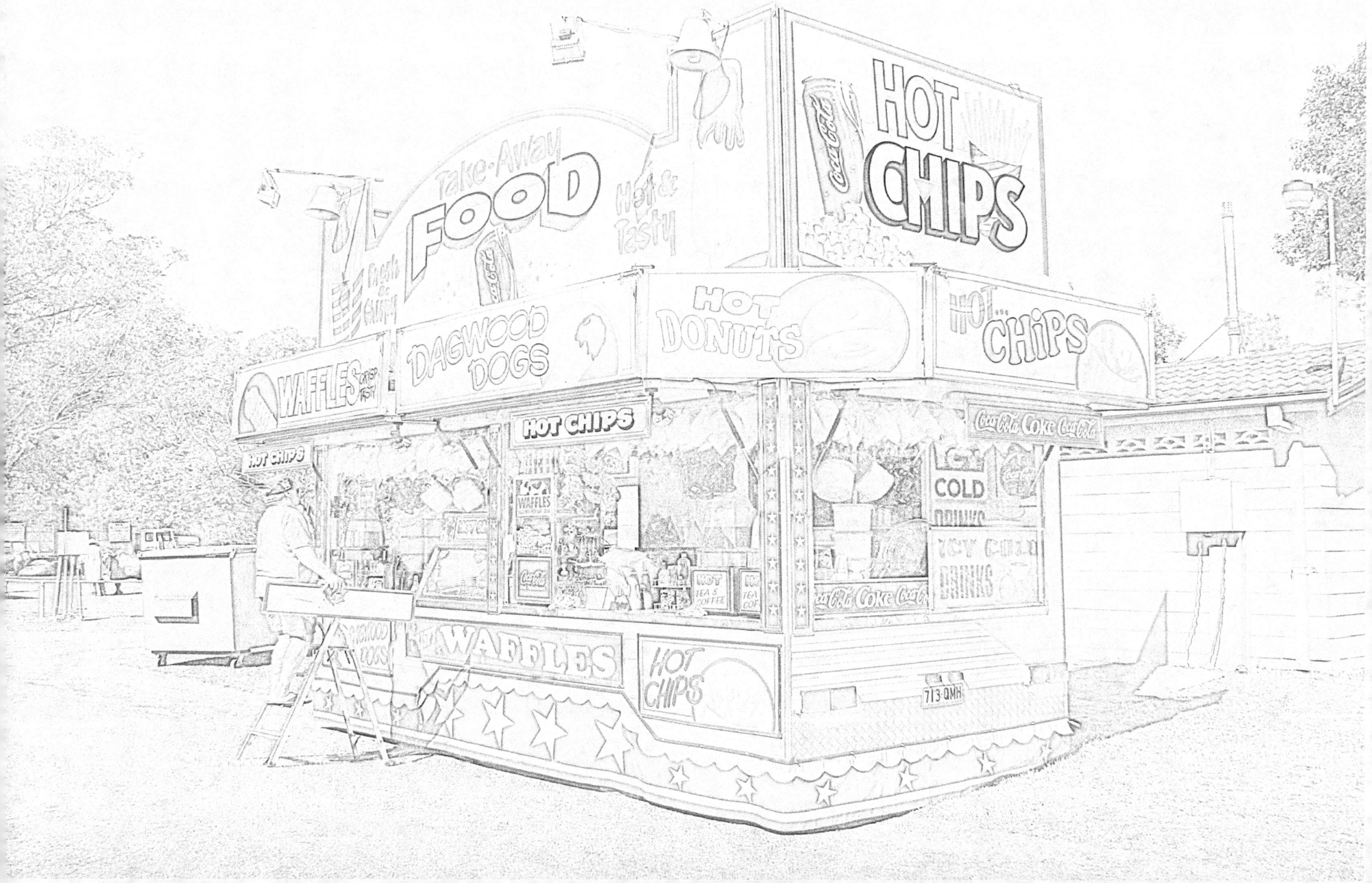
Take-Away
FOOD
Hot & Tasty
Fresh & Crispy
HOT CHIPS
Coca-Cola
WAFFLES CRISP TASTY
DAGWOOD DOGS
HOT DONUTS
HOT... CHIPS
HOT CHIPS
HOT CHIPS
Coca-Cola COKE Coca-Cola
COLD
ICY COLD DRINKS
Coca-Cola COKE Coca-Cola
HOT TEA & COFFEE
WAFFLES
WAFFLES
HOT CHIPS
DAGWOOD DOGS
713·QMH

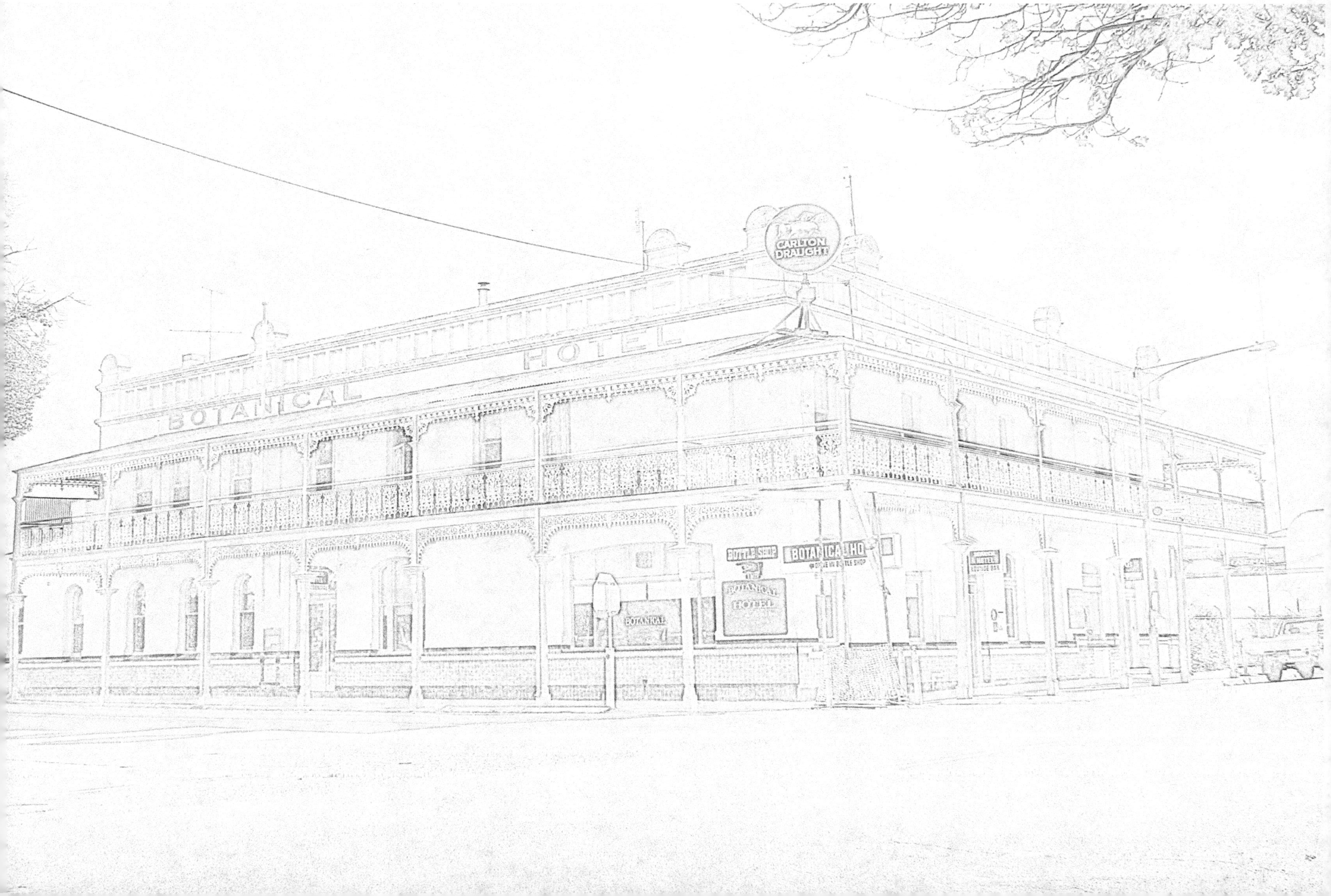
BOTANICAL
HOTEL
CARLTON DRAUGHT
BOTTLE SHOP
BOTANICAL HO
BOTANICAL HOTEL
BOTANICAL
LOUNGE BAR

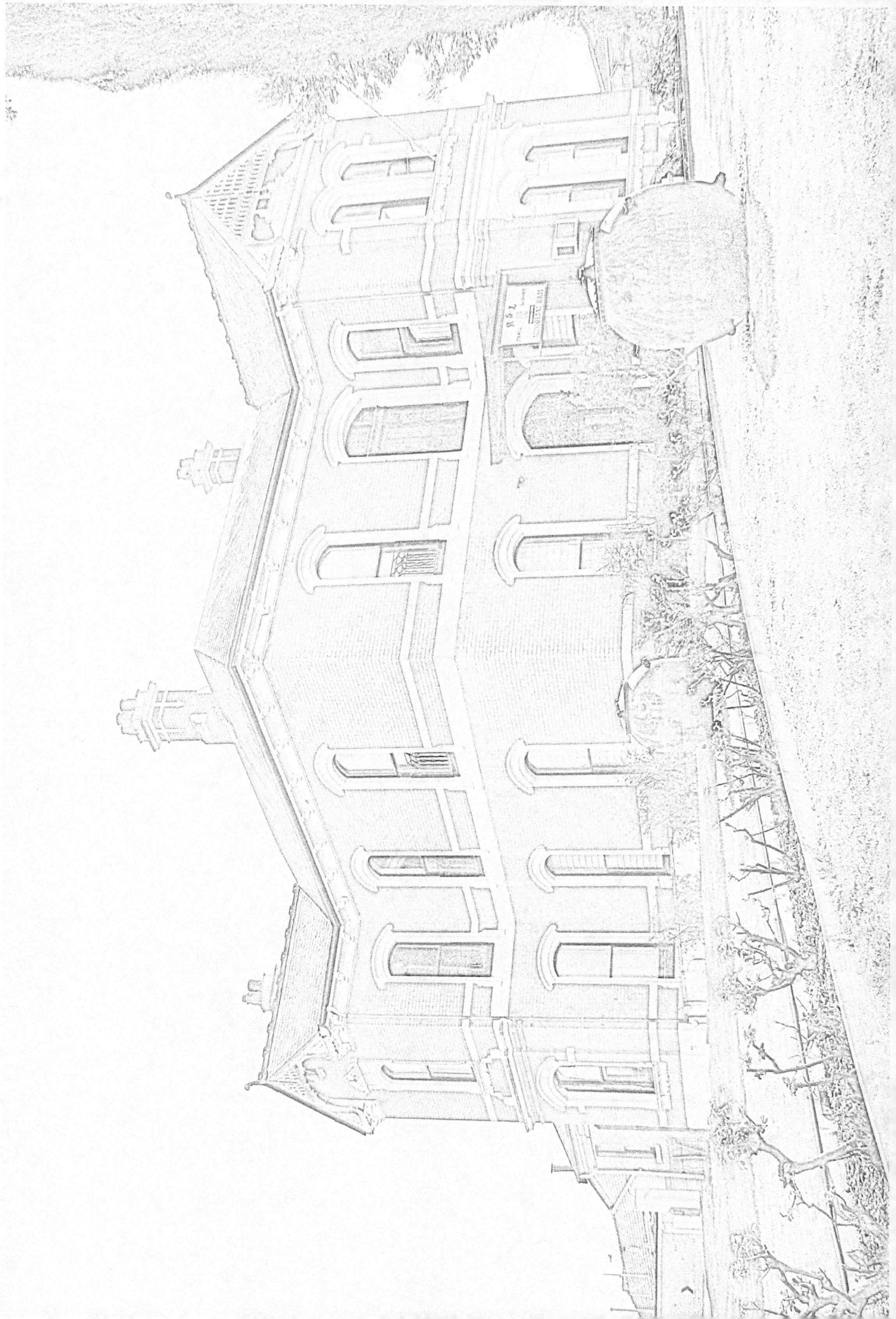
RSL

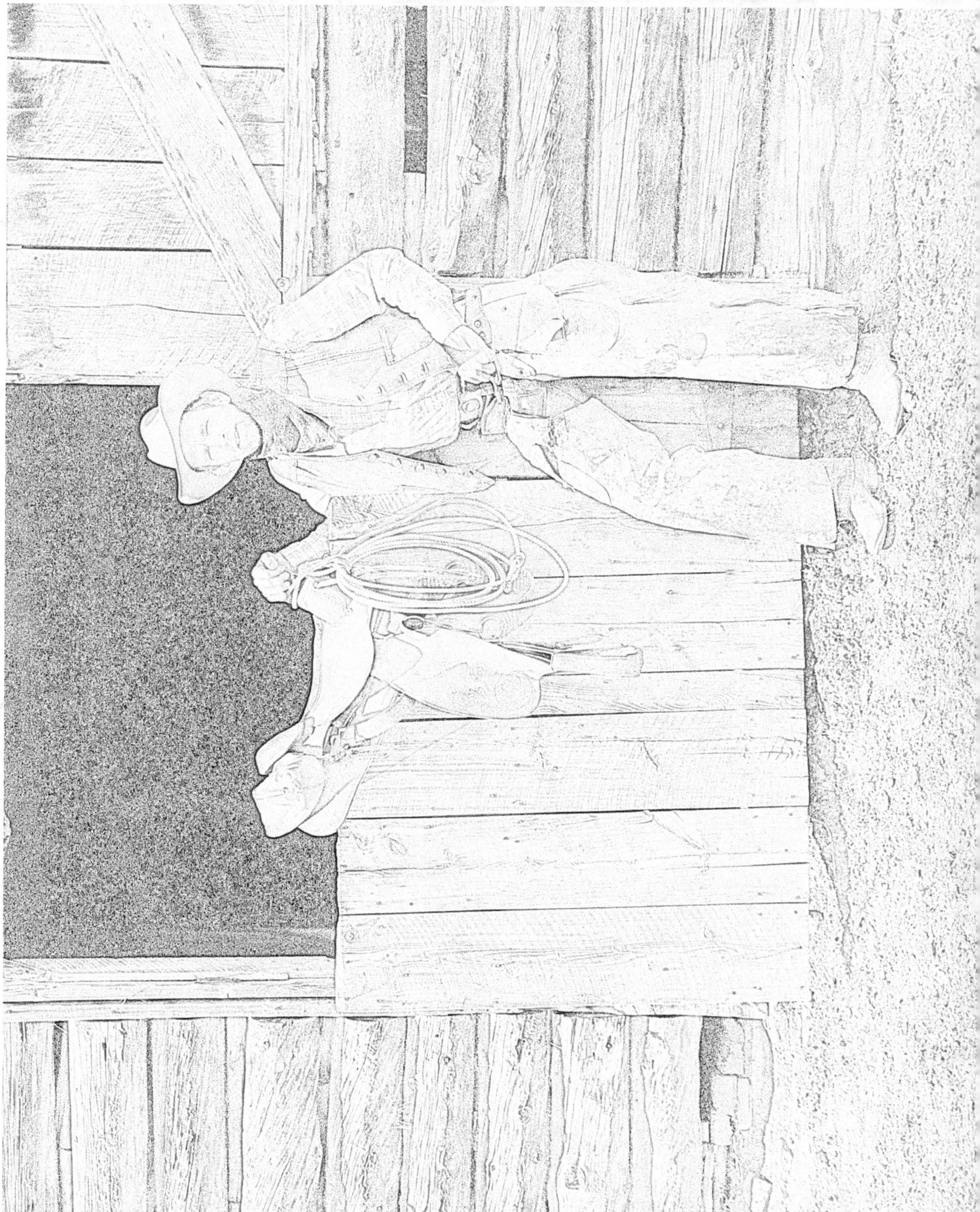

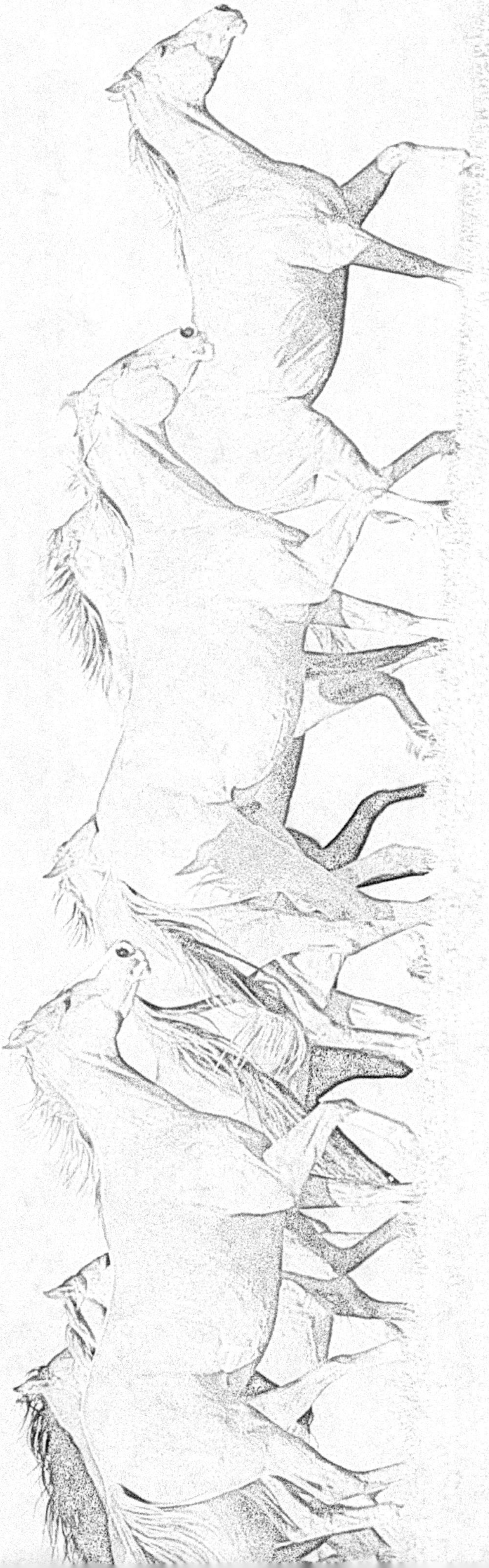

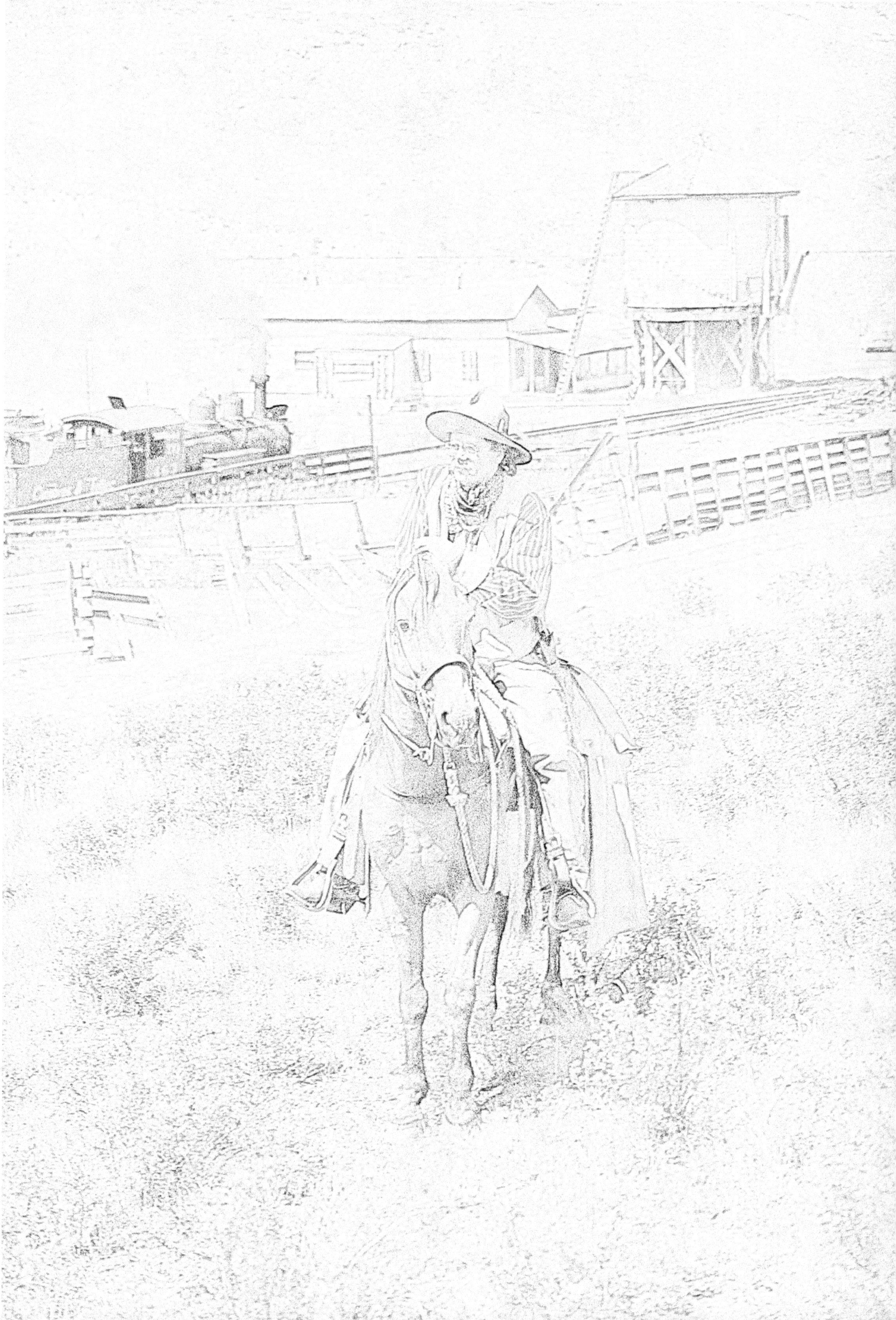

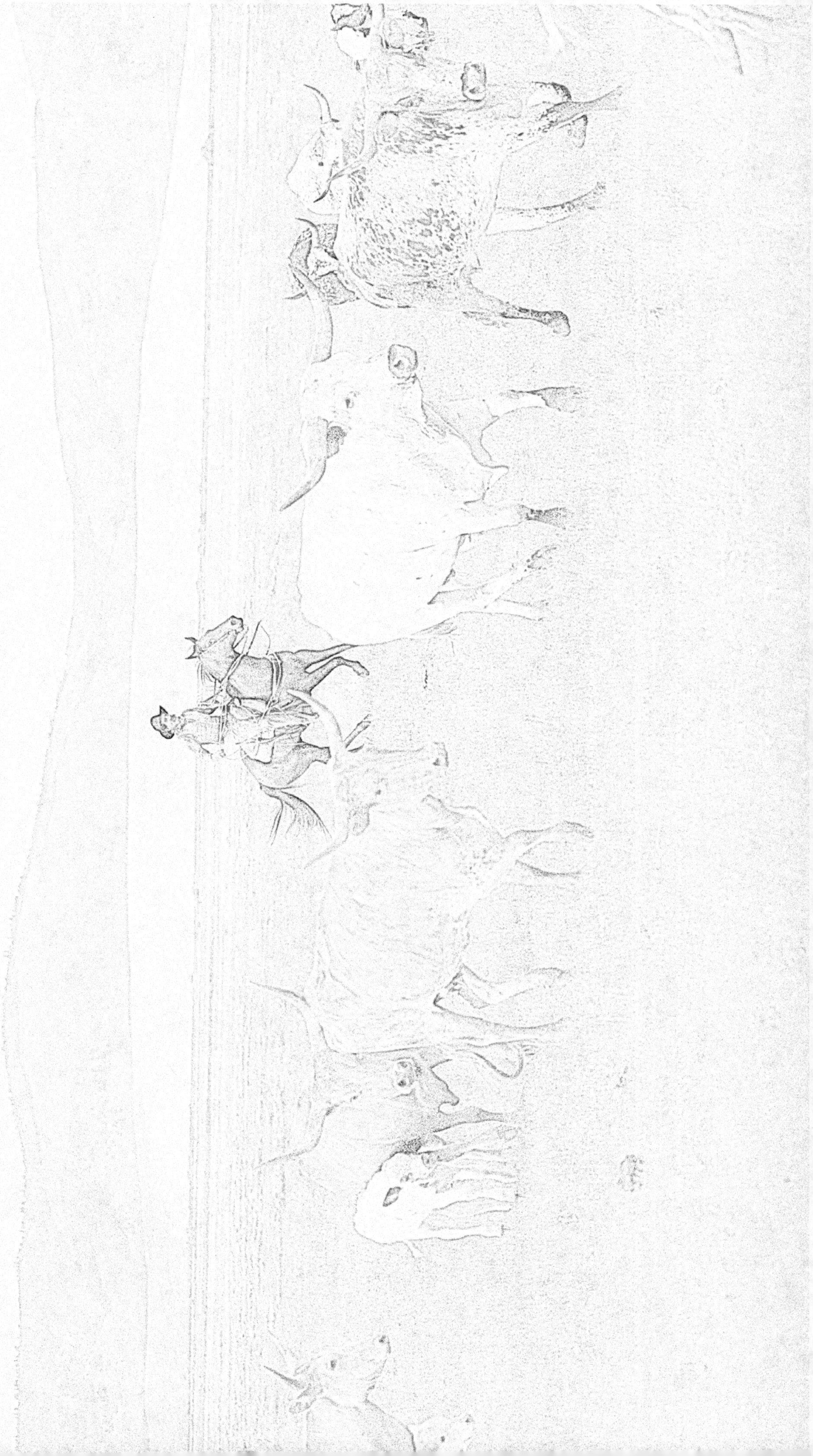

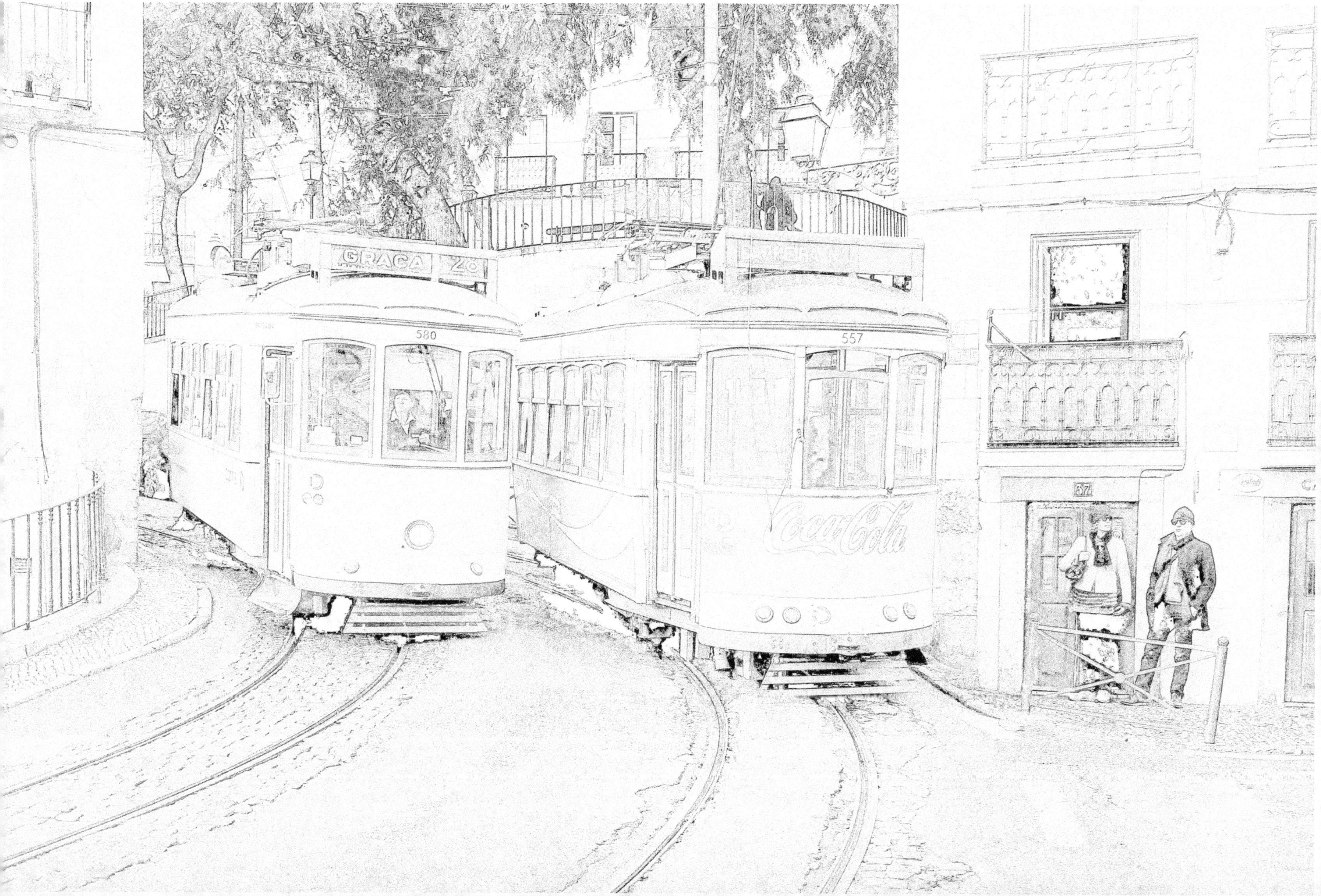
GRAÇA 28
580
557
Coca-Cola
37

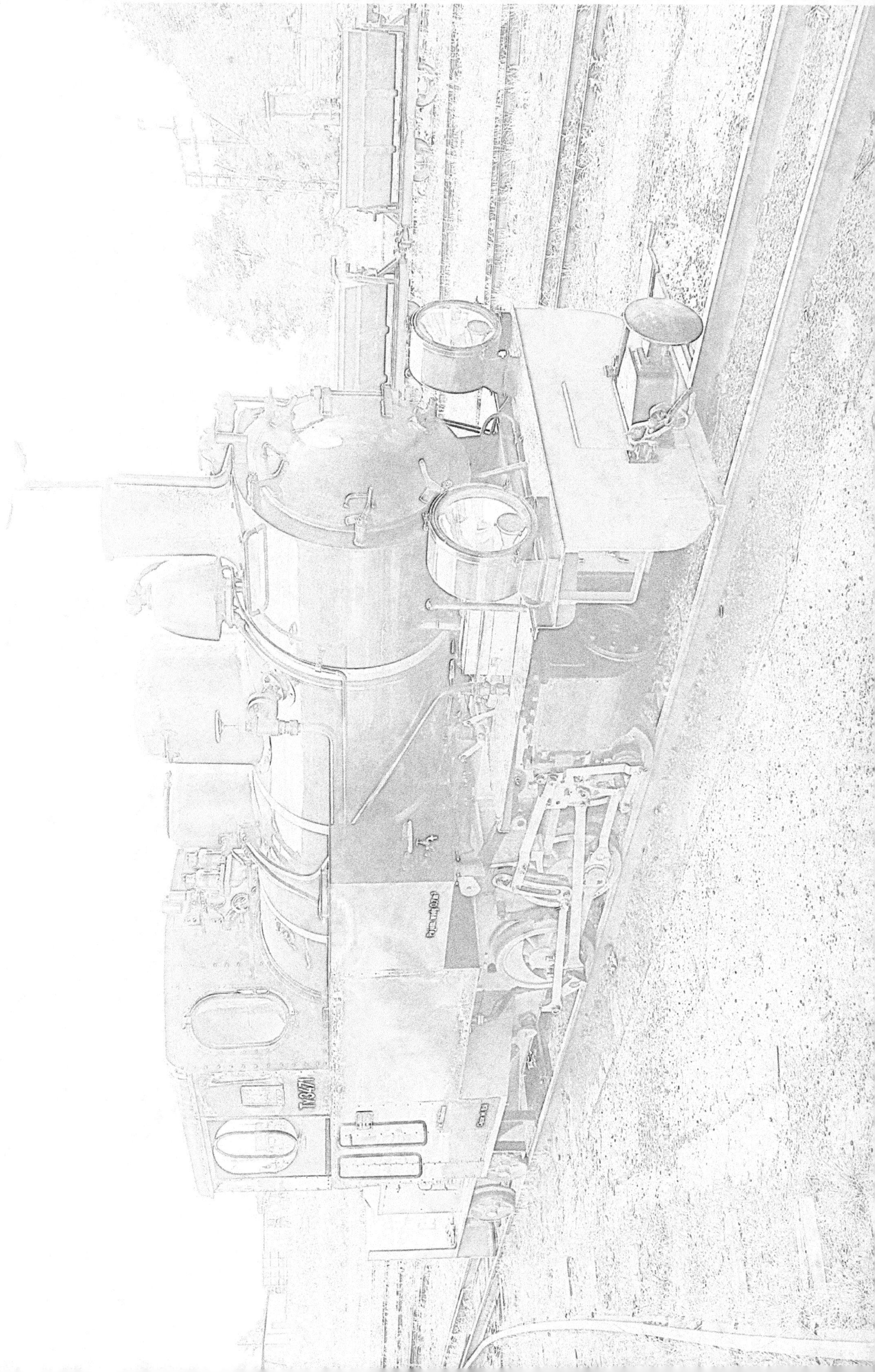

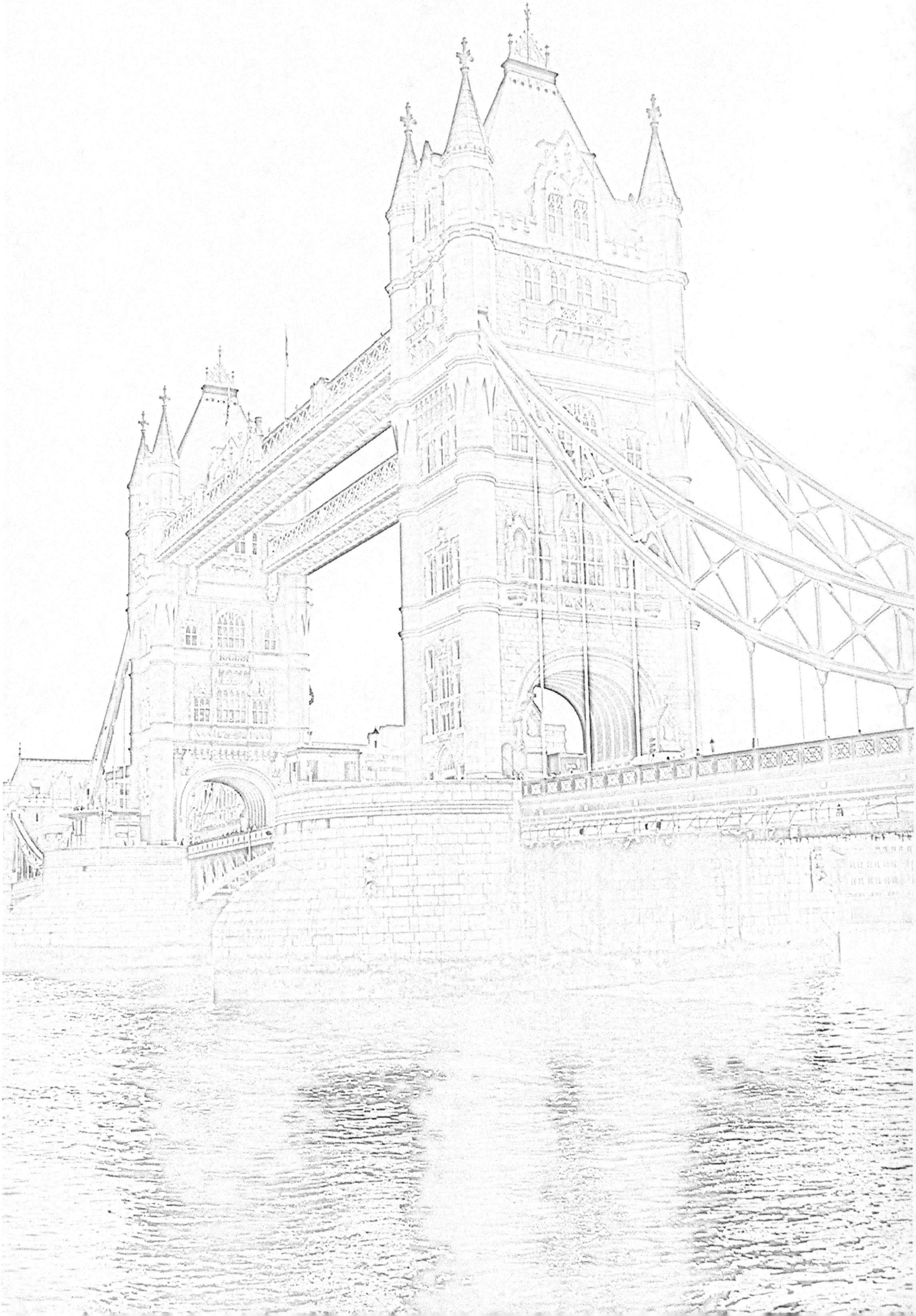

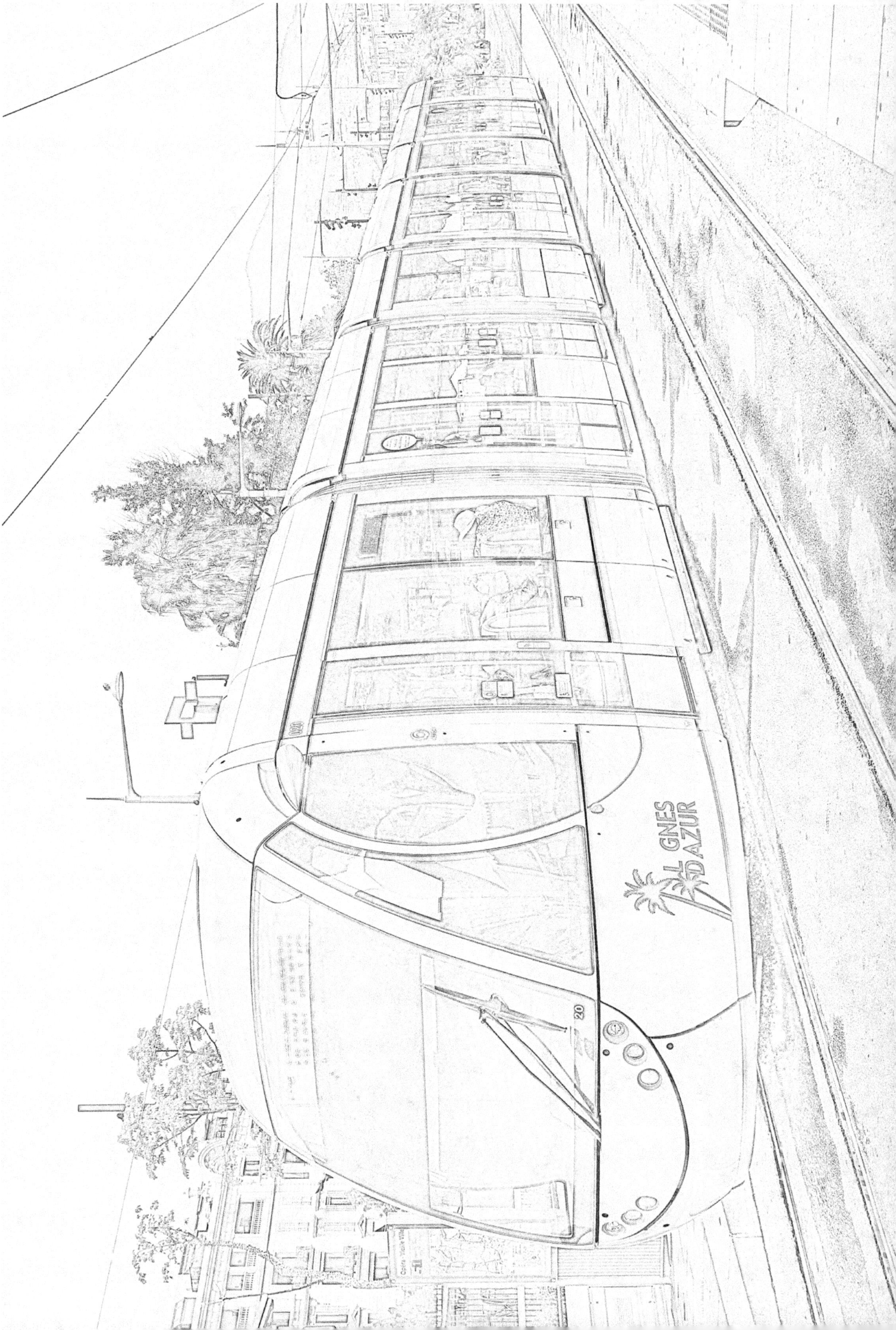
20

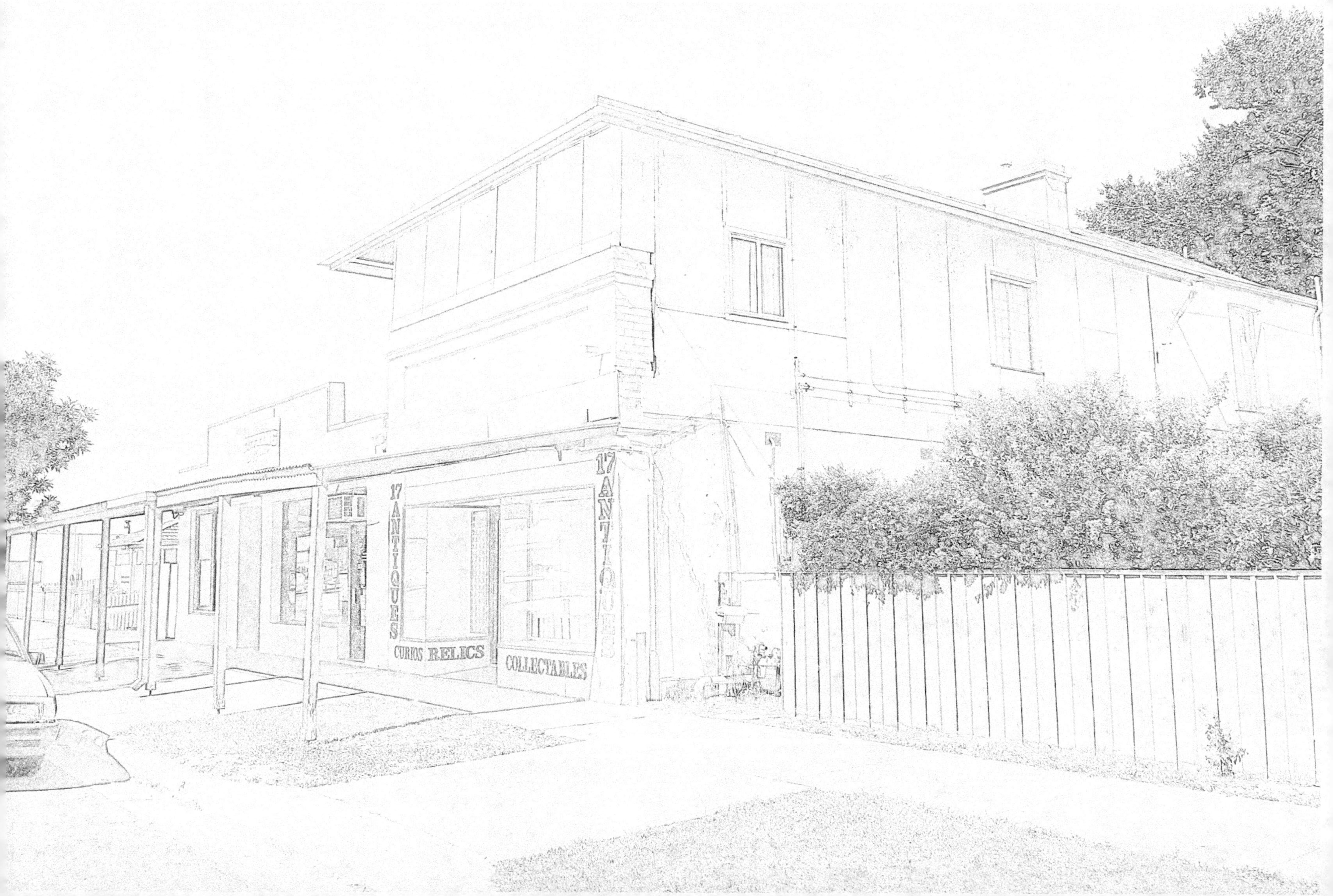
17 ANTIQUES
17 ANTIQUES
CURIOS RELICS
COLLECTABLES

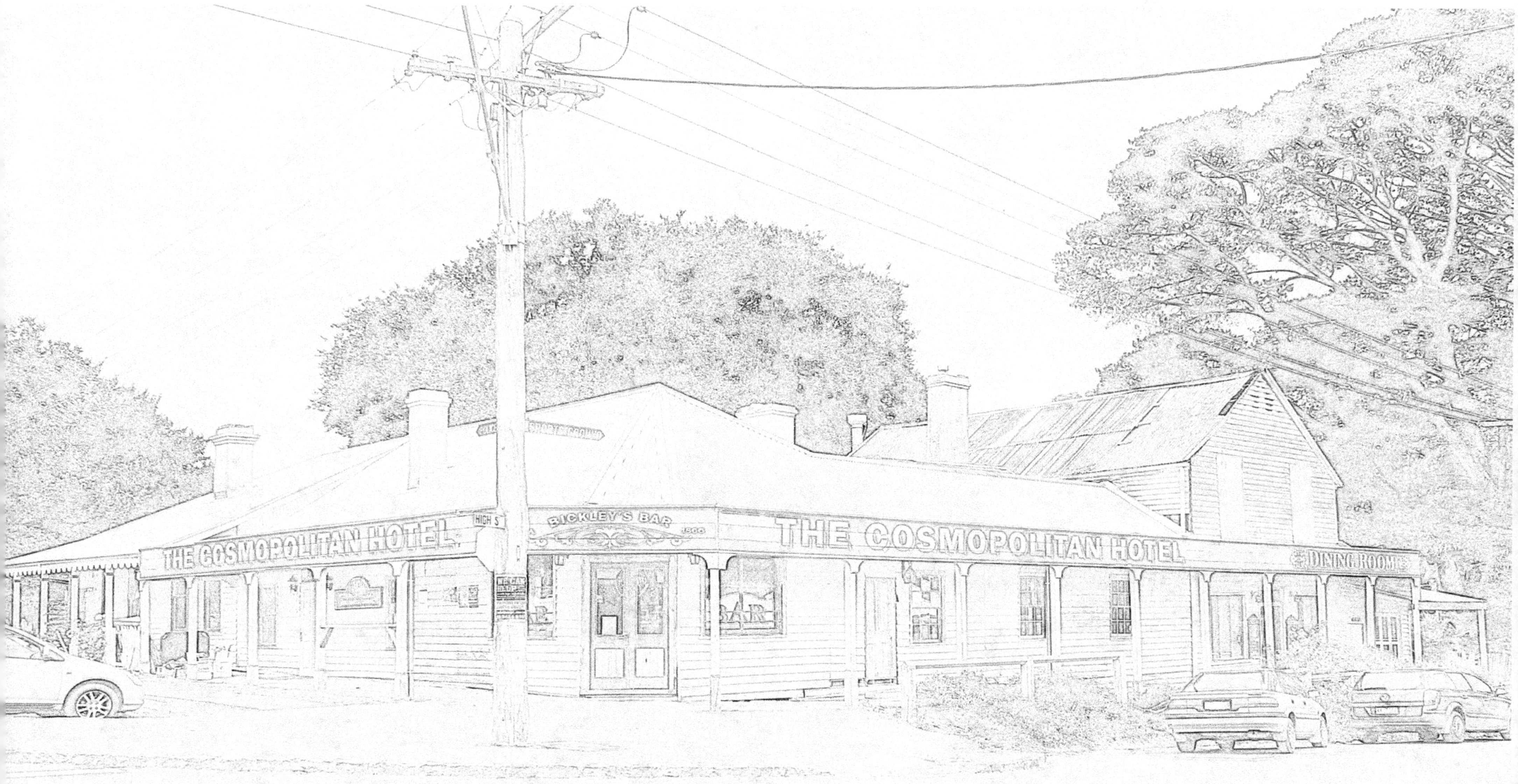
THE COSMOPOLITAN HOTEL
HIGH S
BICKLEY'S BAR
1866
THE COSMOPOLITAN HOTEL
DINING ROOM
BAR

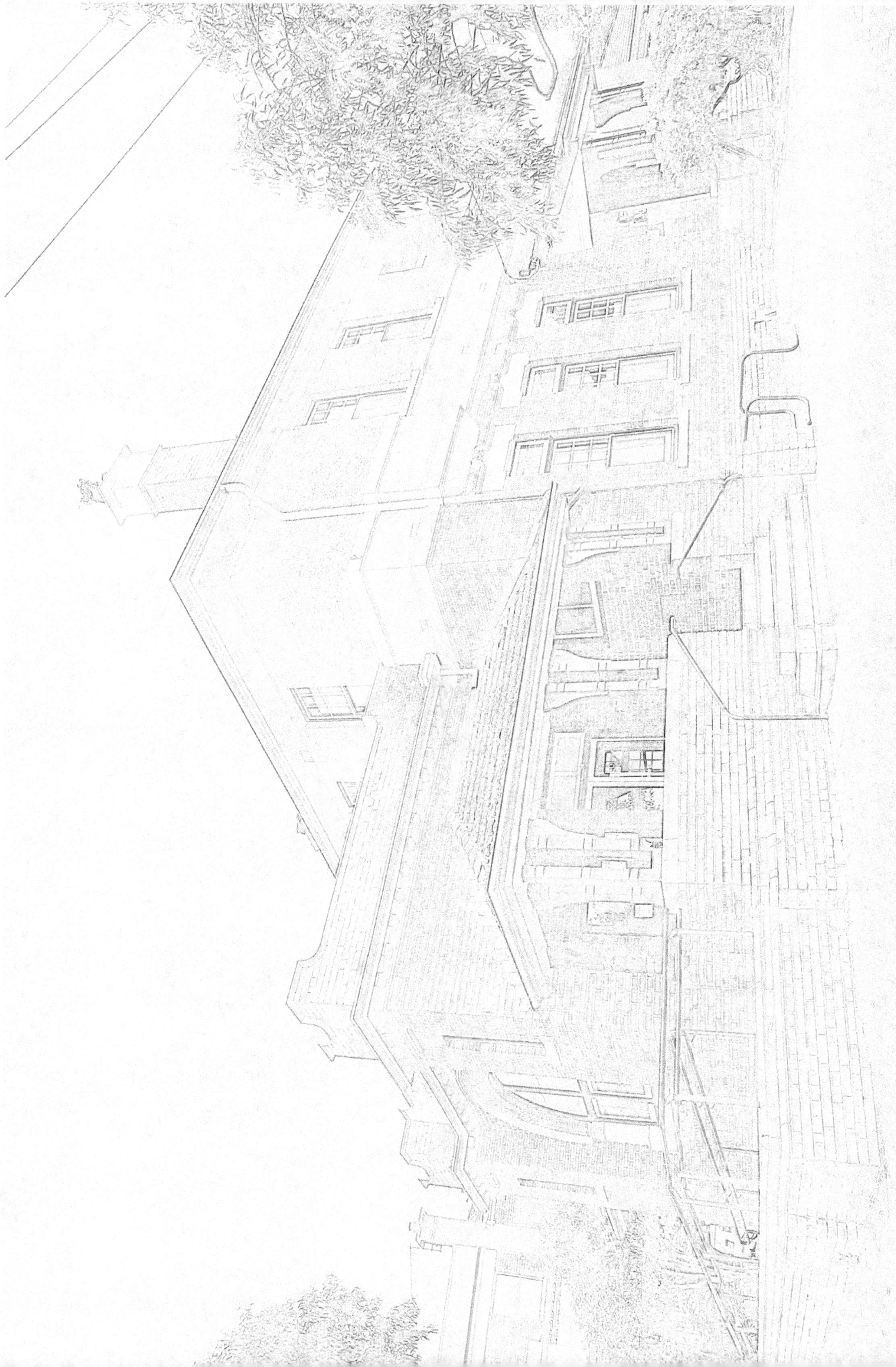

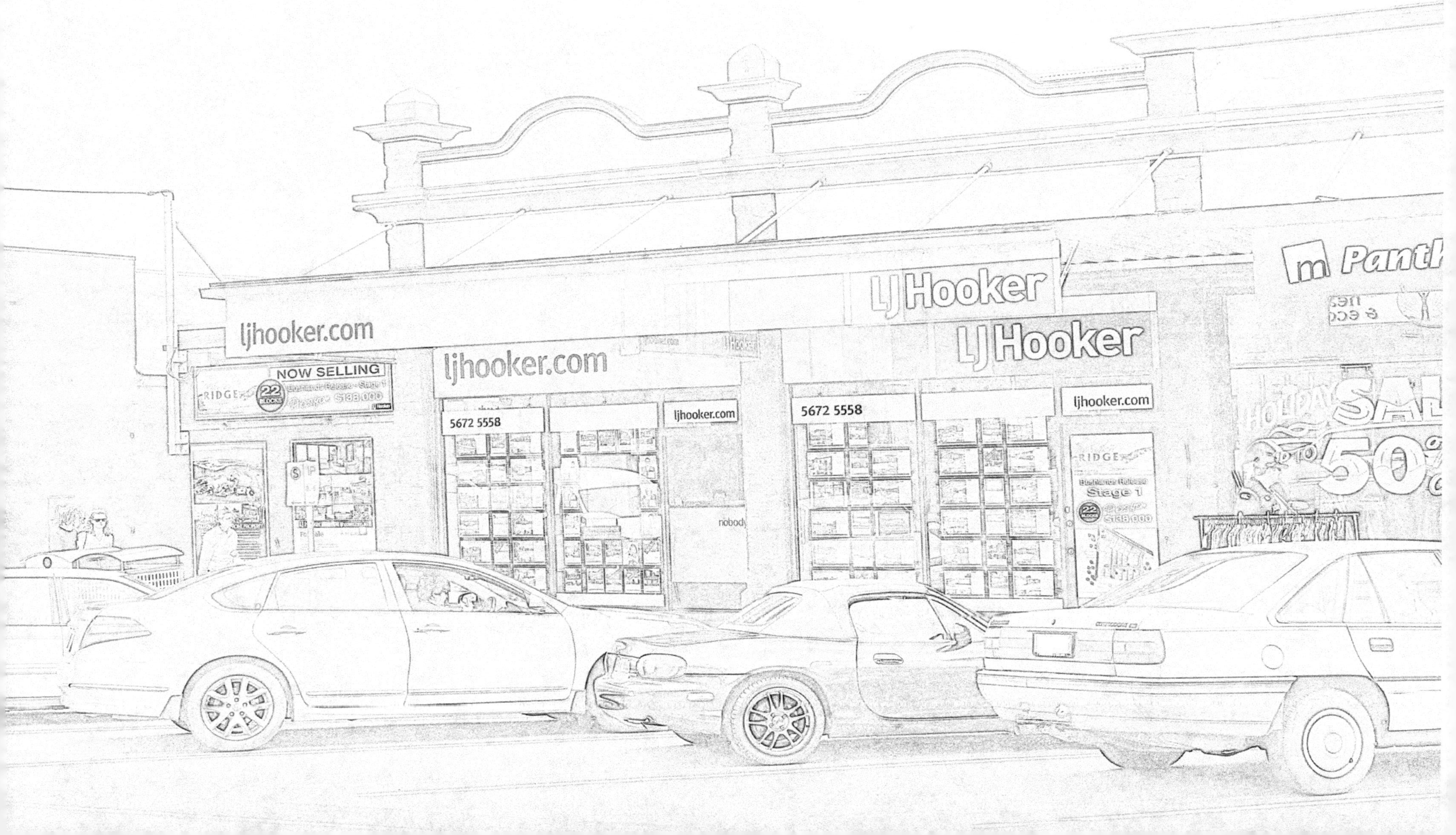
ljhooker.com
NOW SELLING
RIDGE
22 BLOCKS
$188,000
ljhooker.com
5672 5558
ljhooker.com
LJ Hooker
5672 5558
LJ Hooker
ljhooker.com
RIDGE
Stage 1
$188,000
nobody
SALE
50

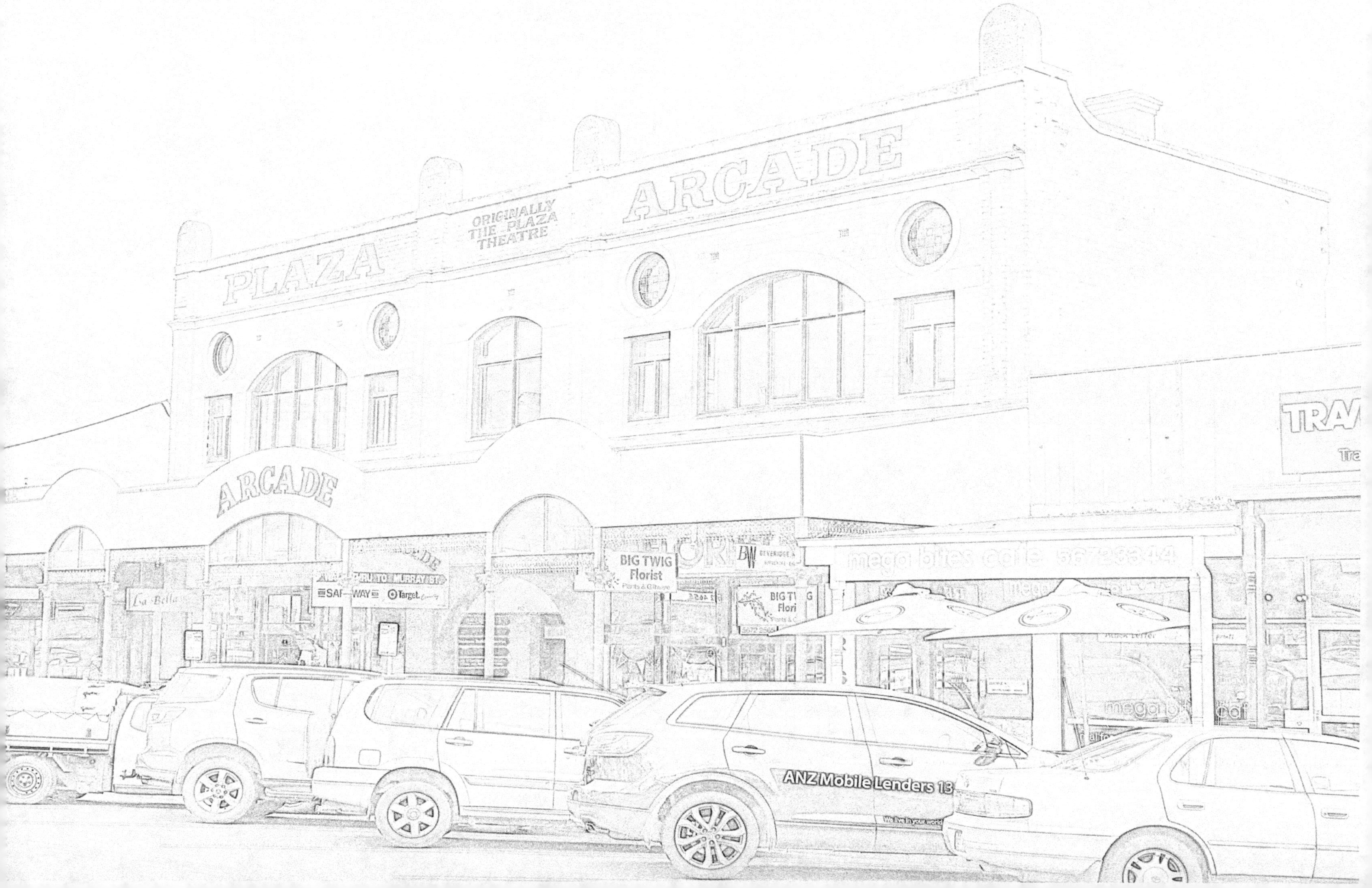
PLAZA
ORIGINALLY THE PLAZA THEATRE
ARCADE
ARCADE
BIG TWIG Florist
Plants & Giftware
SAFEWAY
Target
mega bites cafe
ANZ Mobile Lenders 13
We live in your world

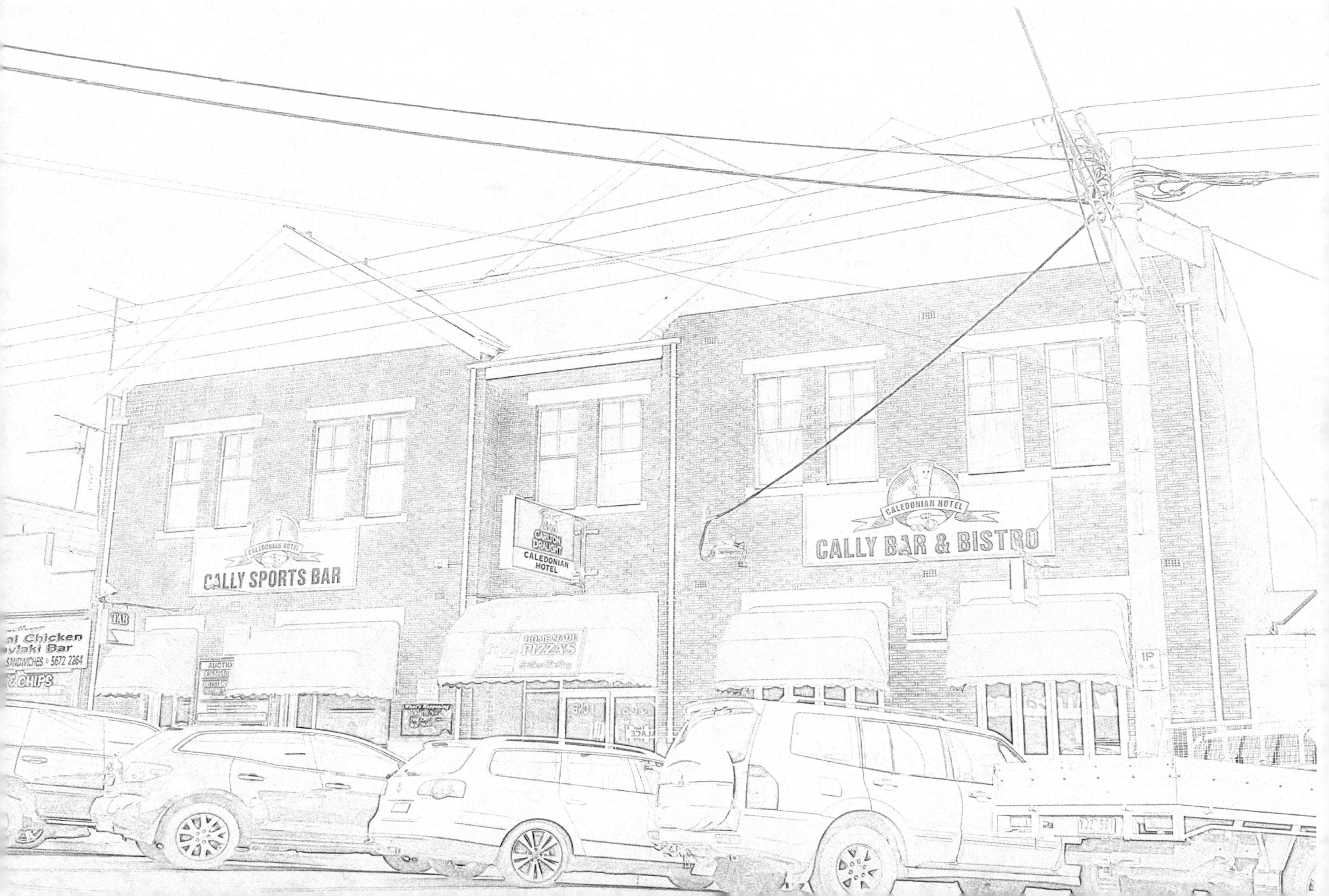
CALEDONIAN HOTEL
CALLY SPORTS BAR
TAB
CARLTON DRAUGHT
CALEDONIAN HOTEL
HOME MADE
PIZZAS
CALEDONIAN HOTEL
CALLY BAR & BISTRO
1P

OPEN
BOOKS
Hand
BOOKS
BASS COAST

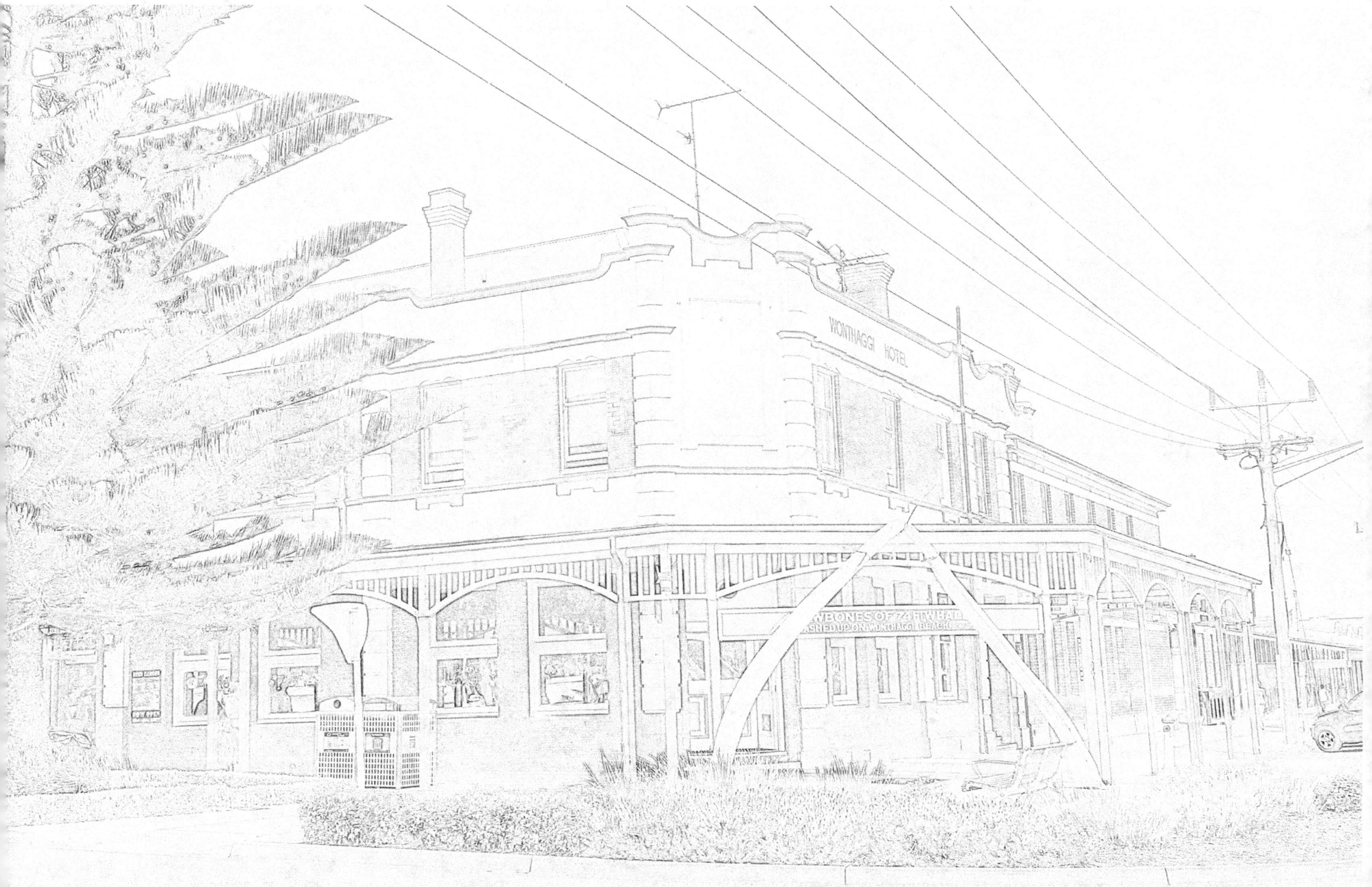
WONTHAGGI HOTEL

RAILWAY STATION
MUSEUM
PARCELS

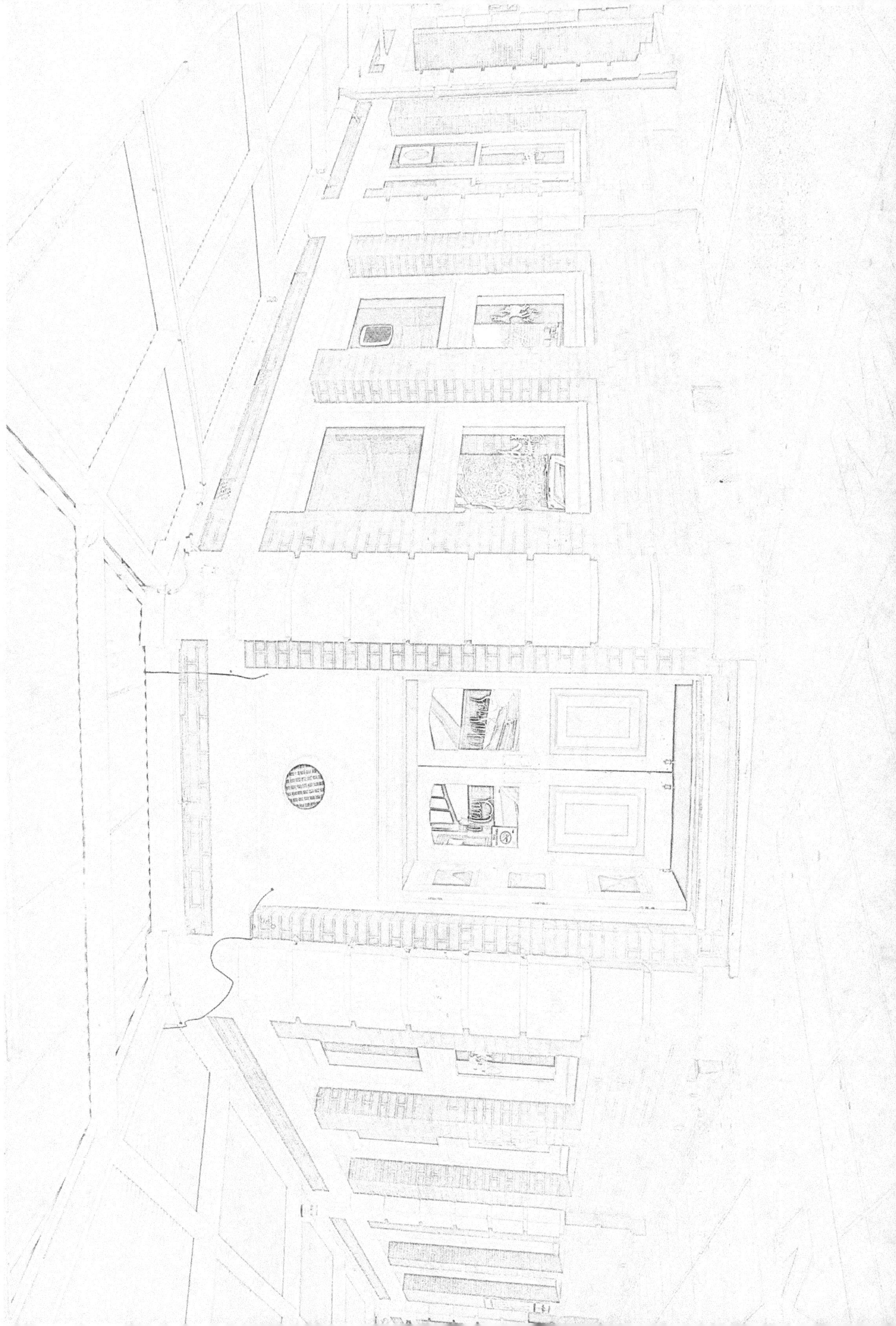

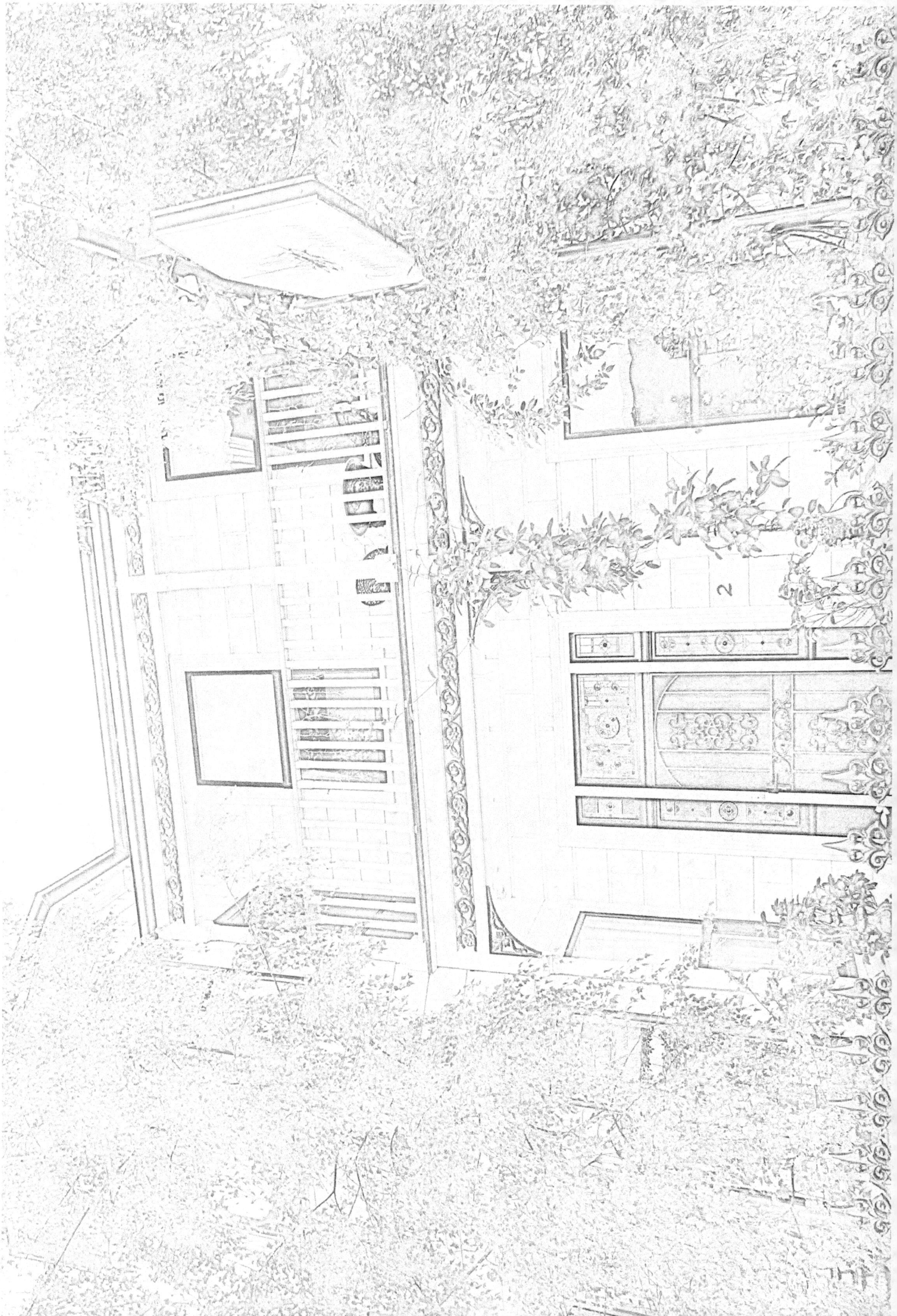

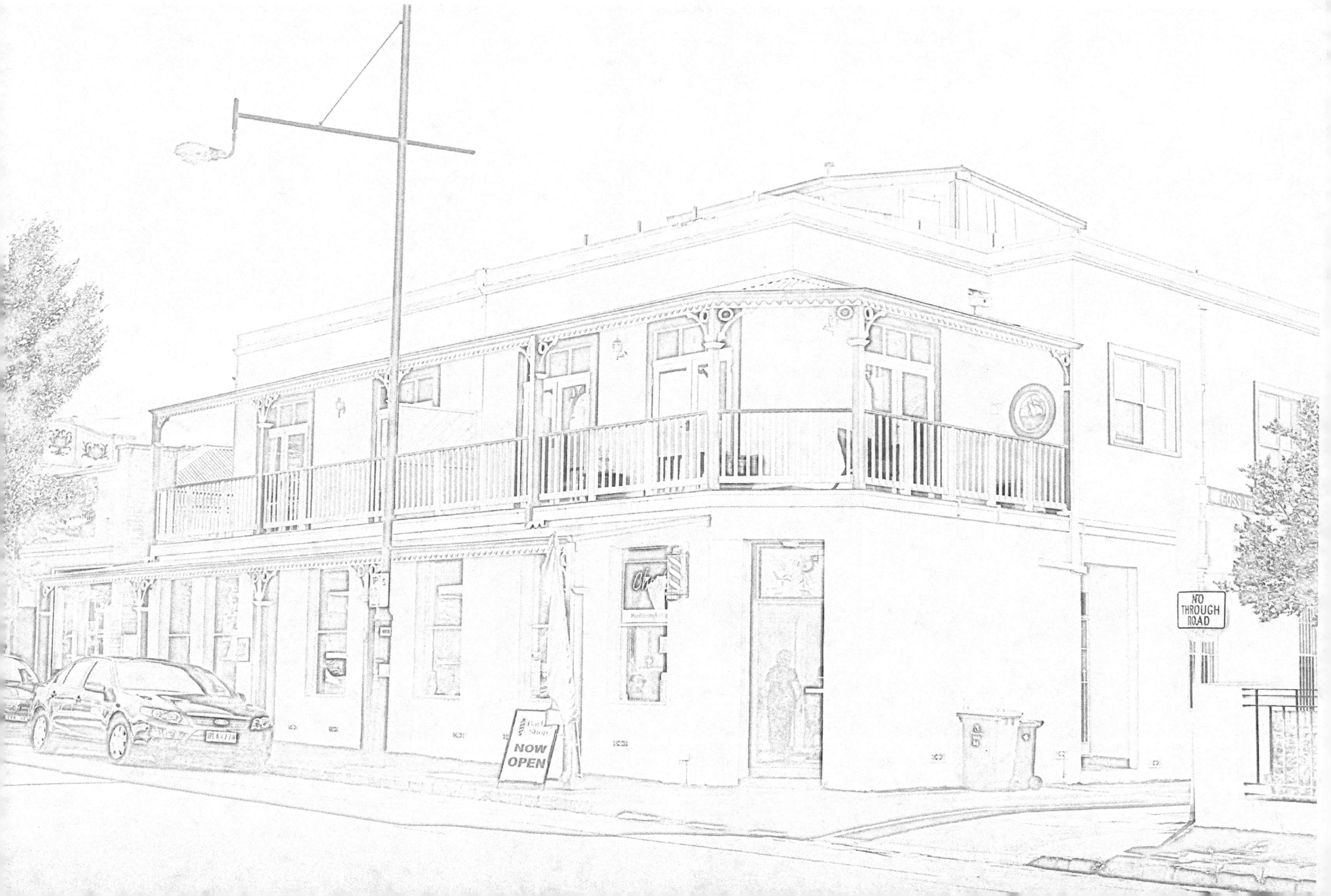
NO
THROUGH
ROAD
NOW
OPEN

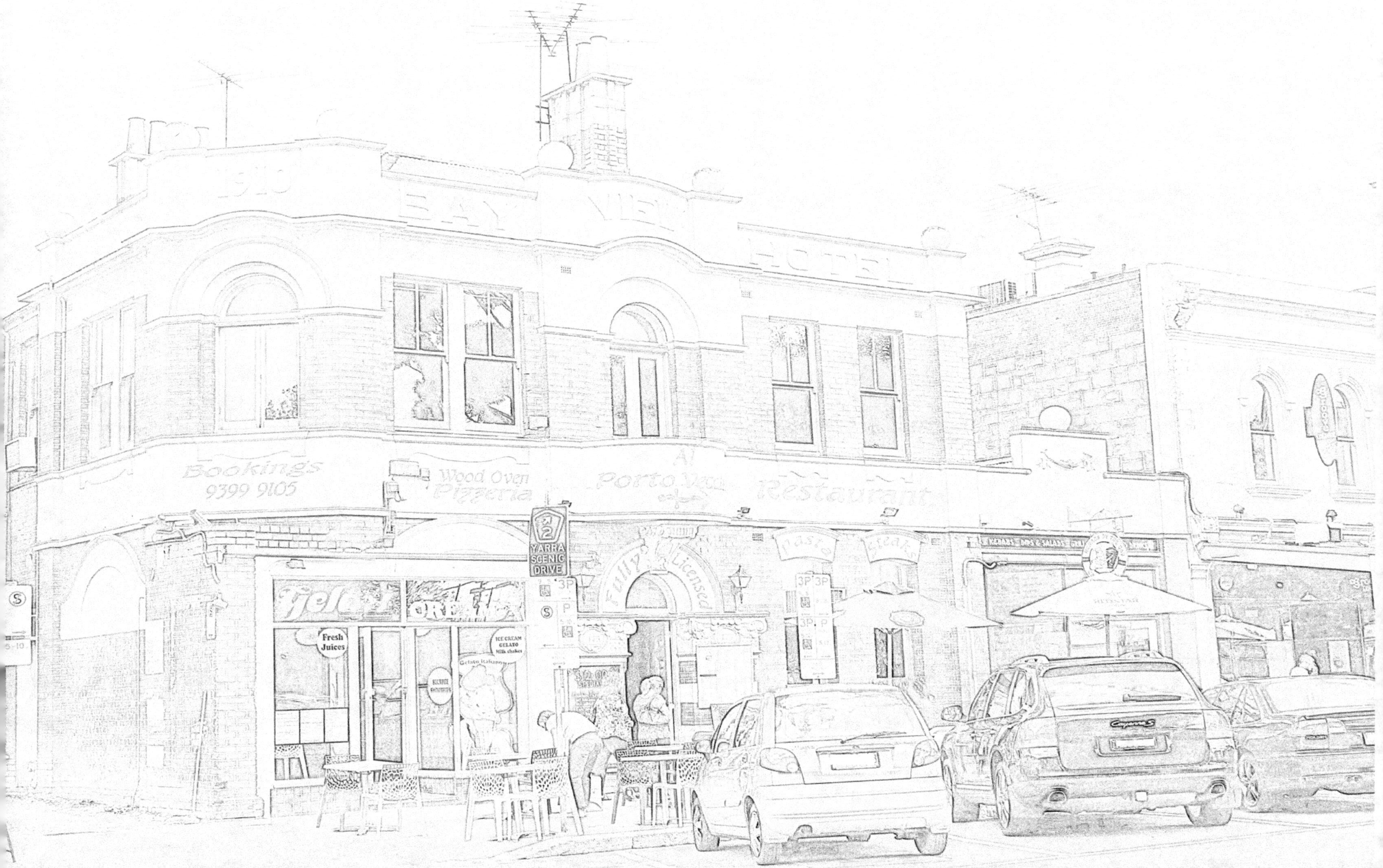
BAY VIEW
HOTEL
Bookings
9399 9105
Wood Oven
Pizzeria
Al
Porto Vecchio
Restaurant
YARRA
SCENIC
DRIVE
Fully Licensed
Pasta
Steaks
Fresh
Juices
ICE CREAM
GELATO
Milk shakes

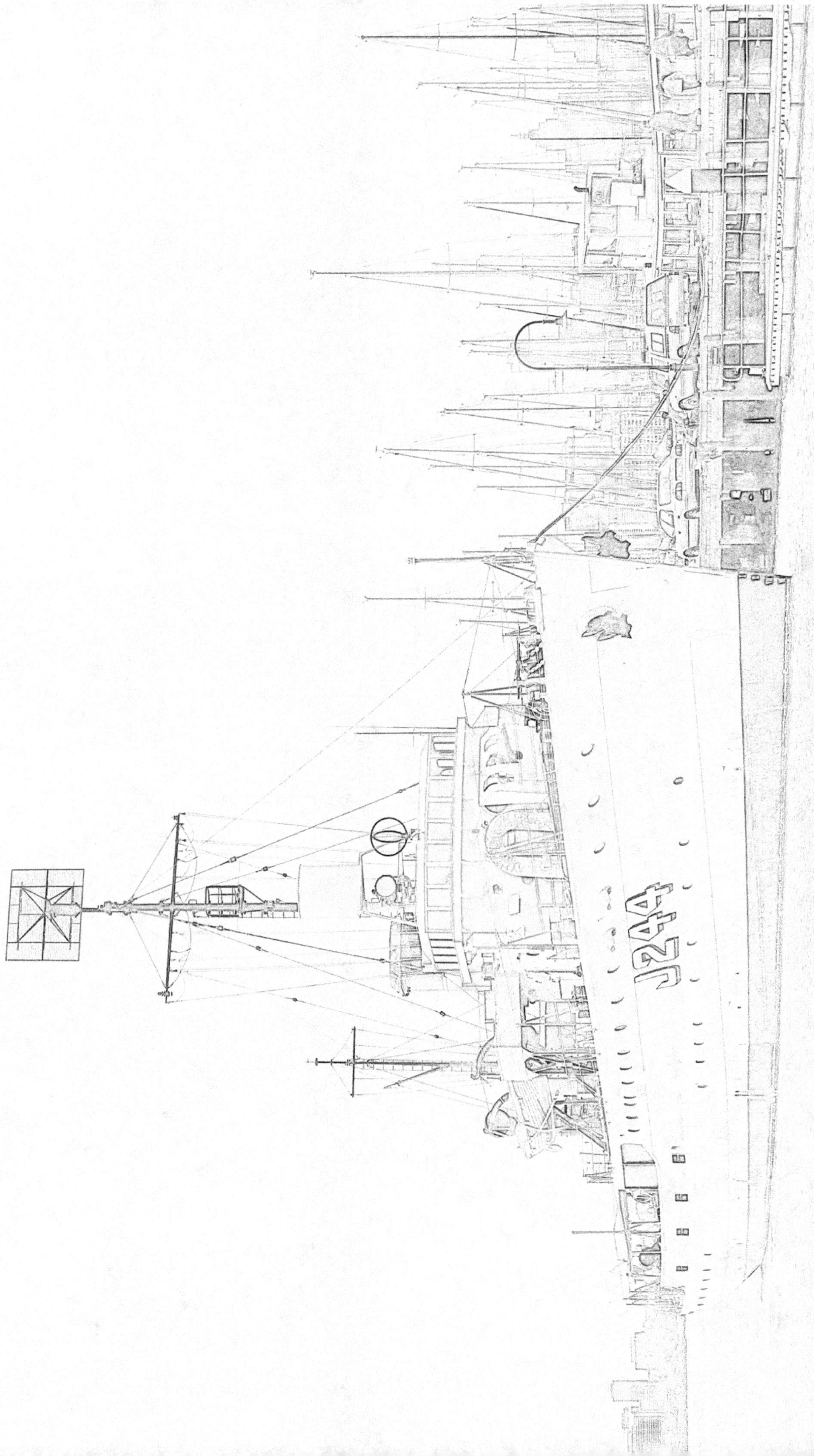
J244

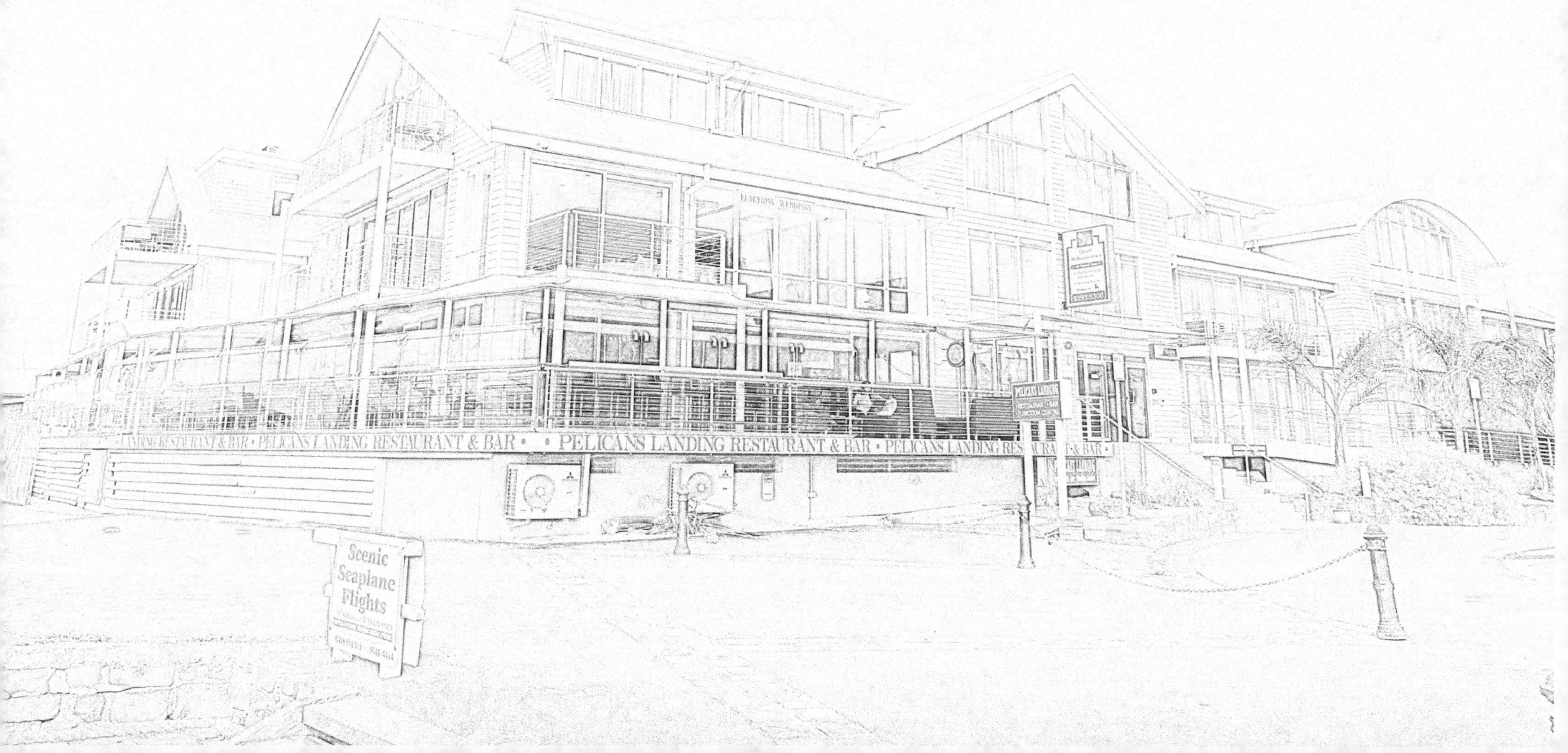

FUNCTIONS WEDDINGS
PELICANS LANDING RESTAURANT & BAR • PELICANS LANDING RESTAURANT & BAR • PELICANS LANDING RESTAURANT & BAR
Scenic
Seaplane
Flights

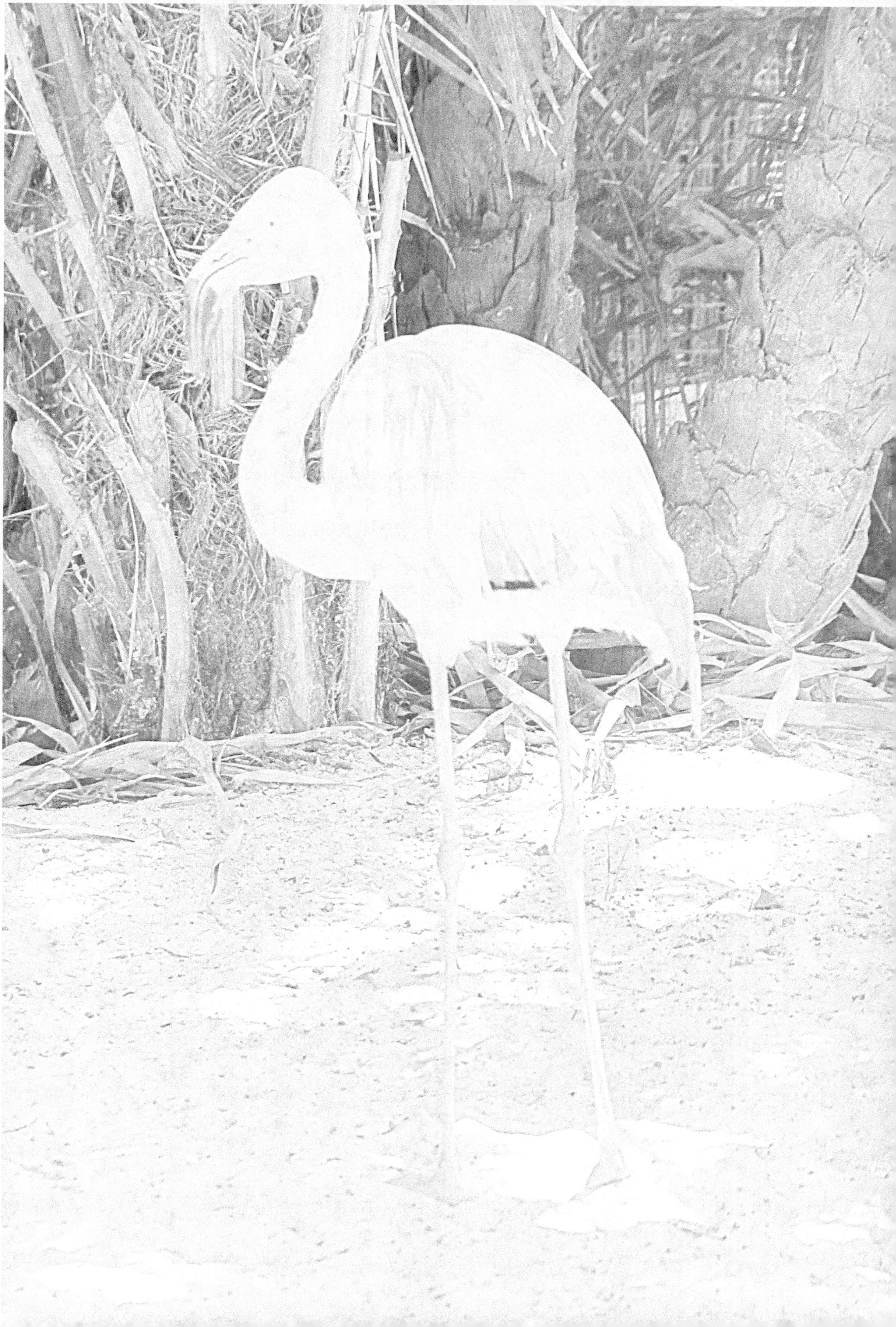

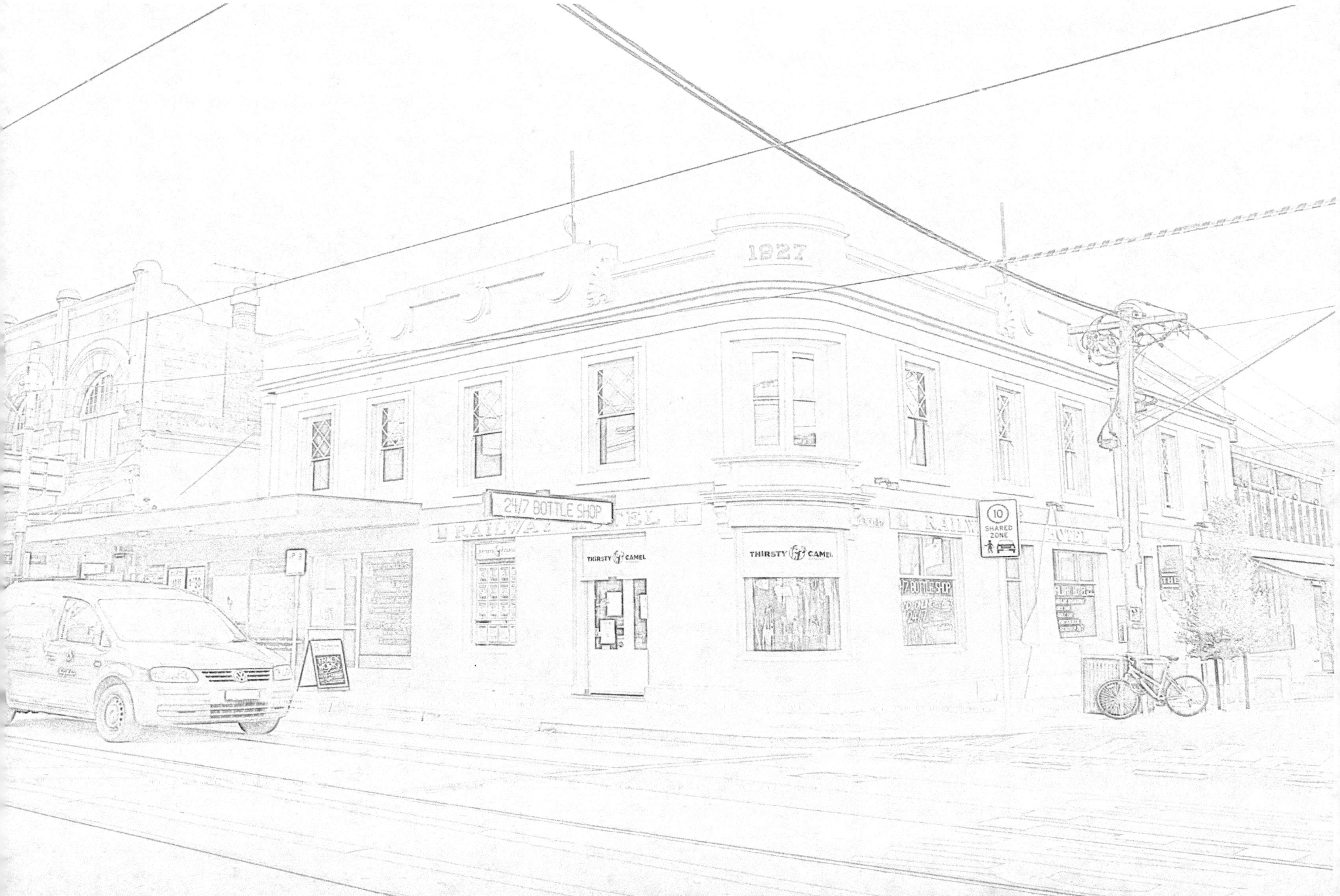
1927
24/7 BOTTLE SHOP
RAILWAY HOTEL
THIRSTY CAMEL
THIRSTY CAMEL
10
SHARED ZONE

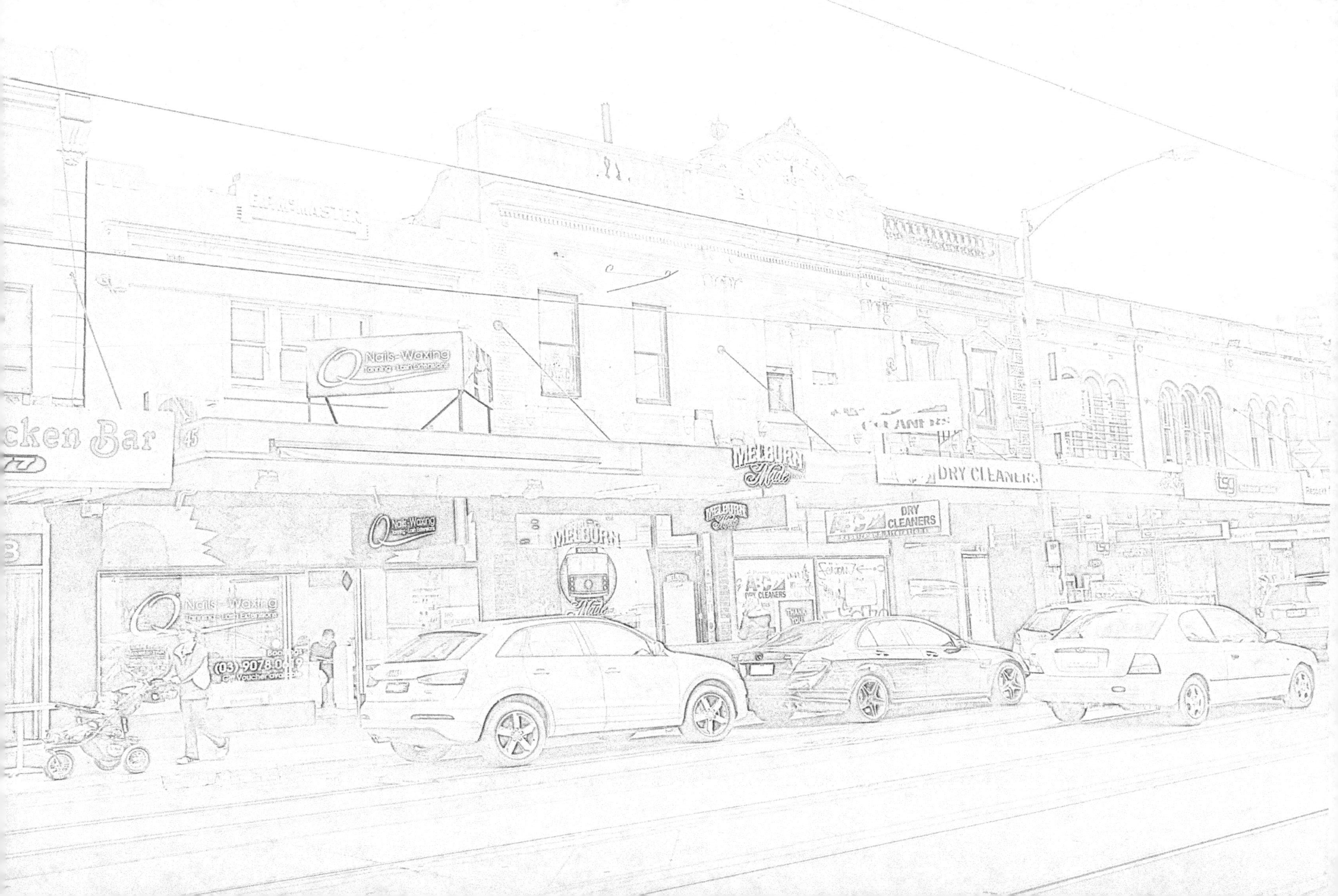
cken Bar
45
Nails-Waxing
MELBURN Male
DRY CLEANERS
DRY CLEANERS
(03) 9078

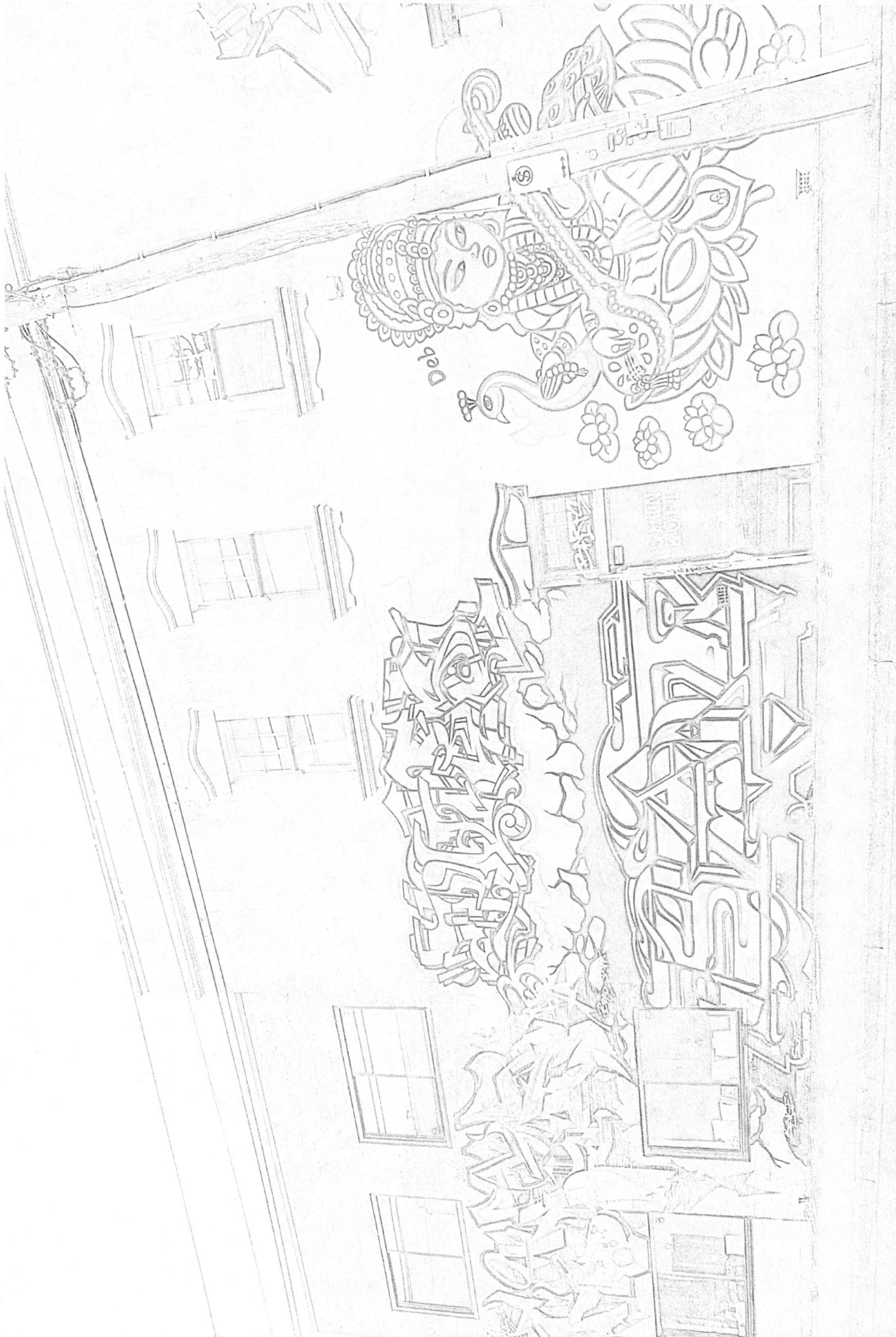
Deb

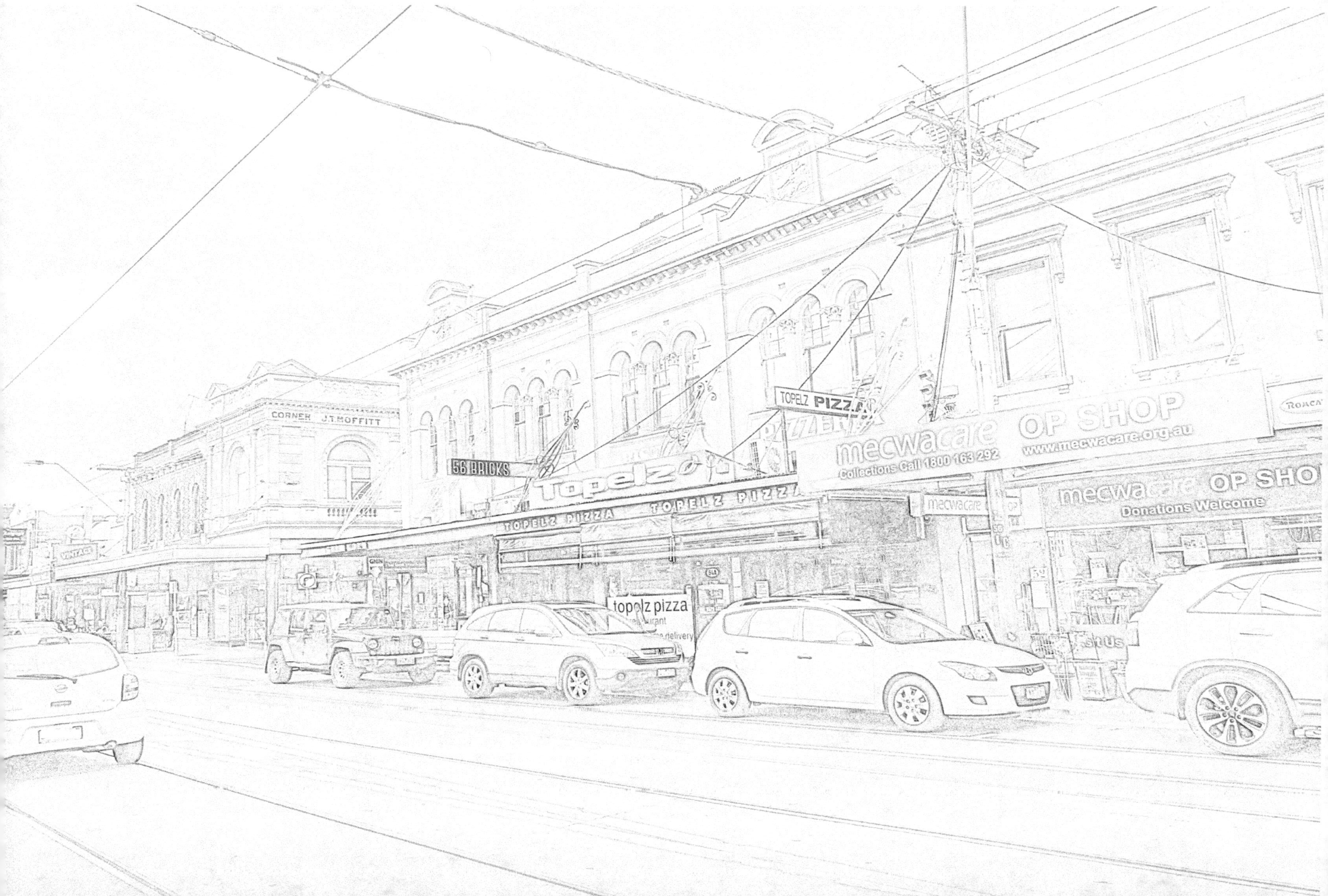
CORNER J.T.MOFFITT
VINTAGE
56 BRICKS
Topelz
TOPELZ PIZZA
TOPELZ PIZZA
TOPELZ PIZZA
topelz pizza
mecwacare OP SHOP
www.mecwacare.org.au
Collections Call 1800 163 292
mecwacare
mecwacare OP SHOP
Donations Welcome

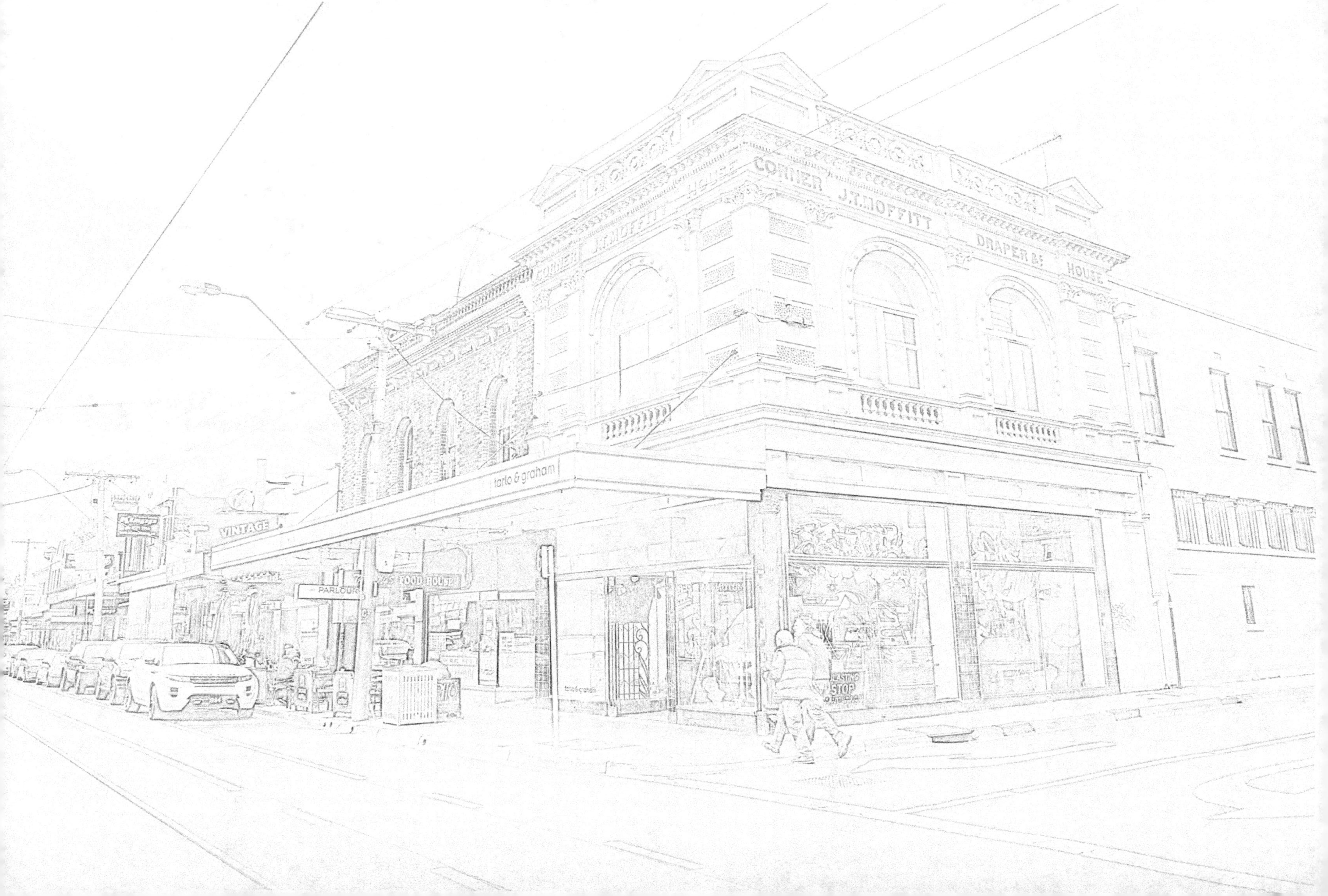
CORNER
J.T.MOFFITT
DRAPER &
HOUSE
tarlo & graham
VINTAGE
PARLOUR
FOOD HOUSE
STOP

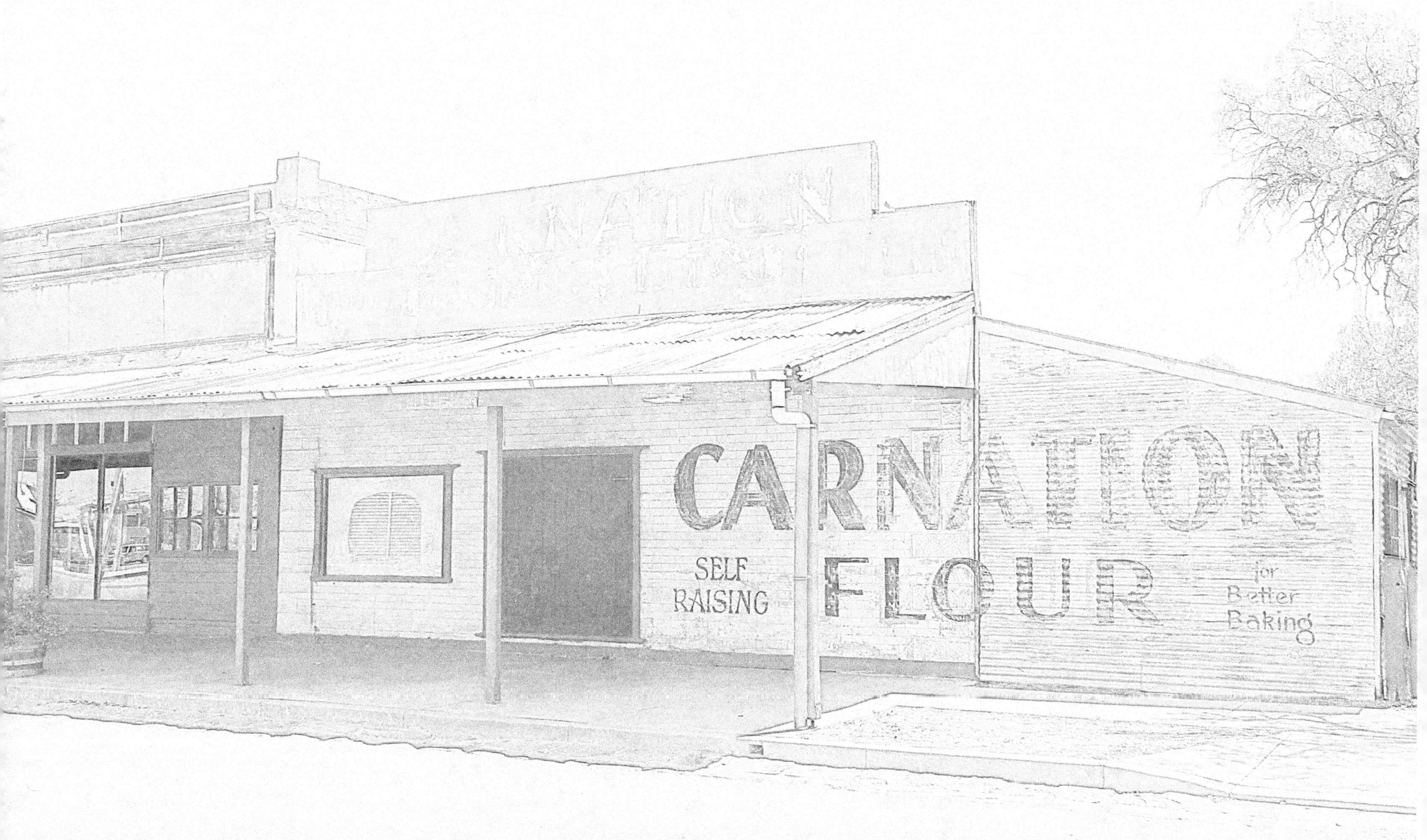
CARNATION
SELF RAISING
FLOUR
for Better Baking

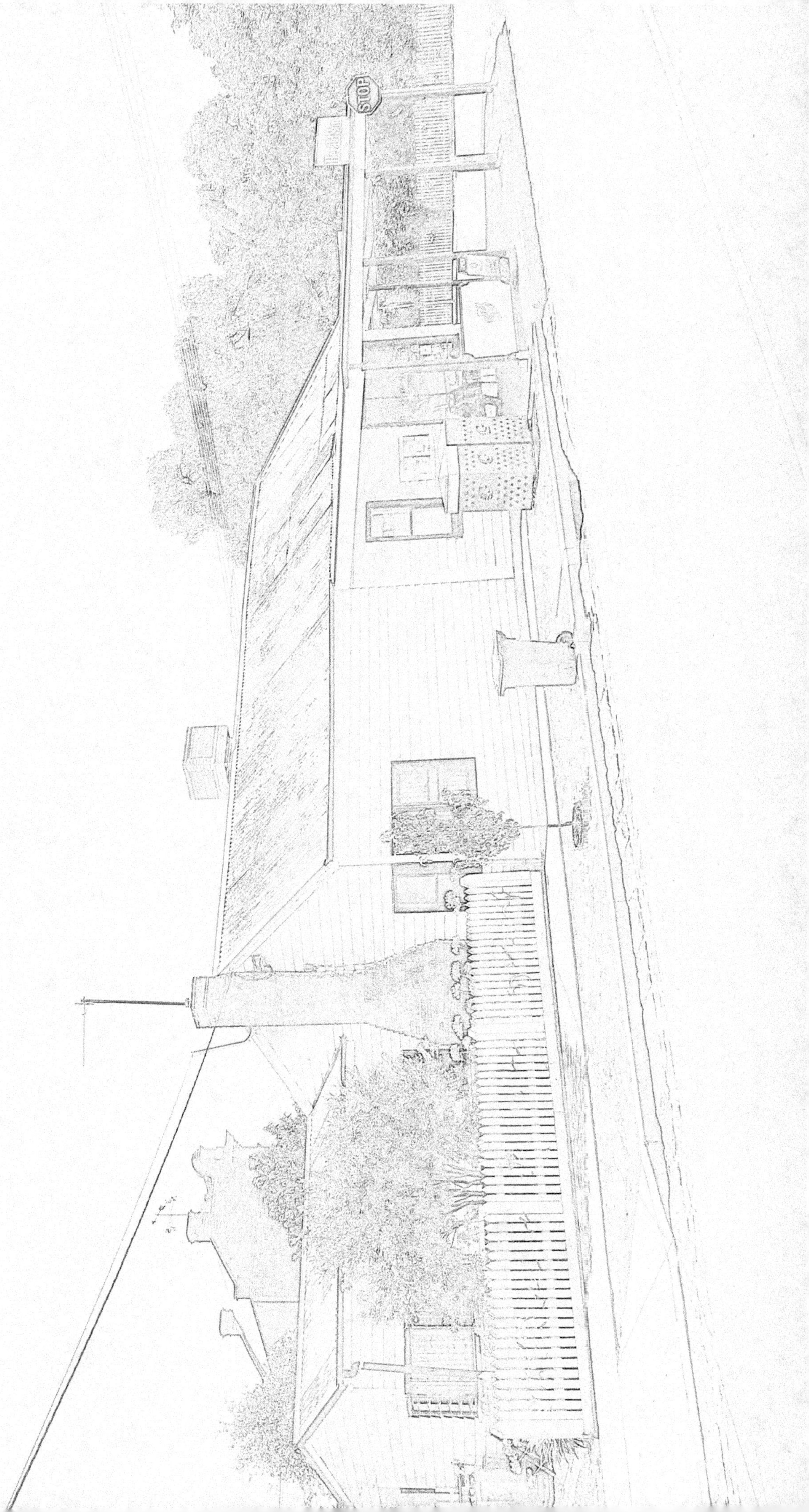
STOP

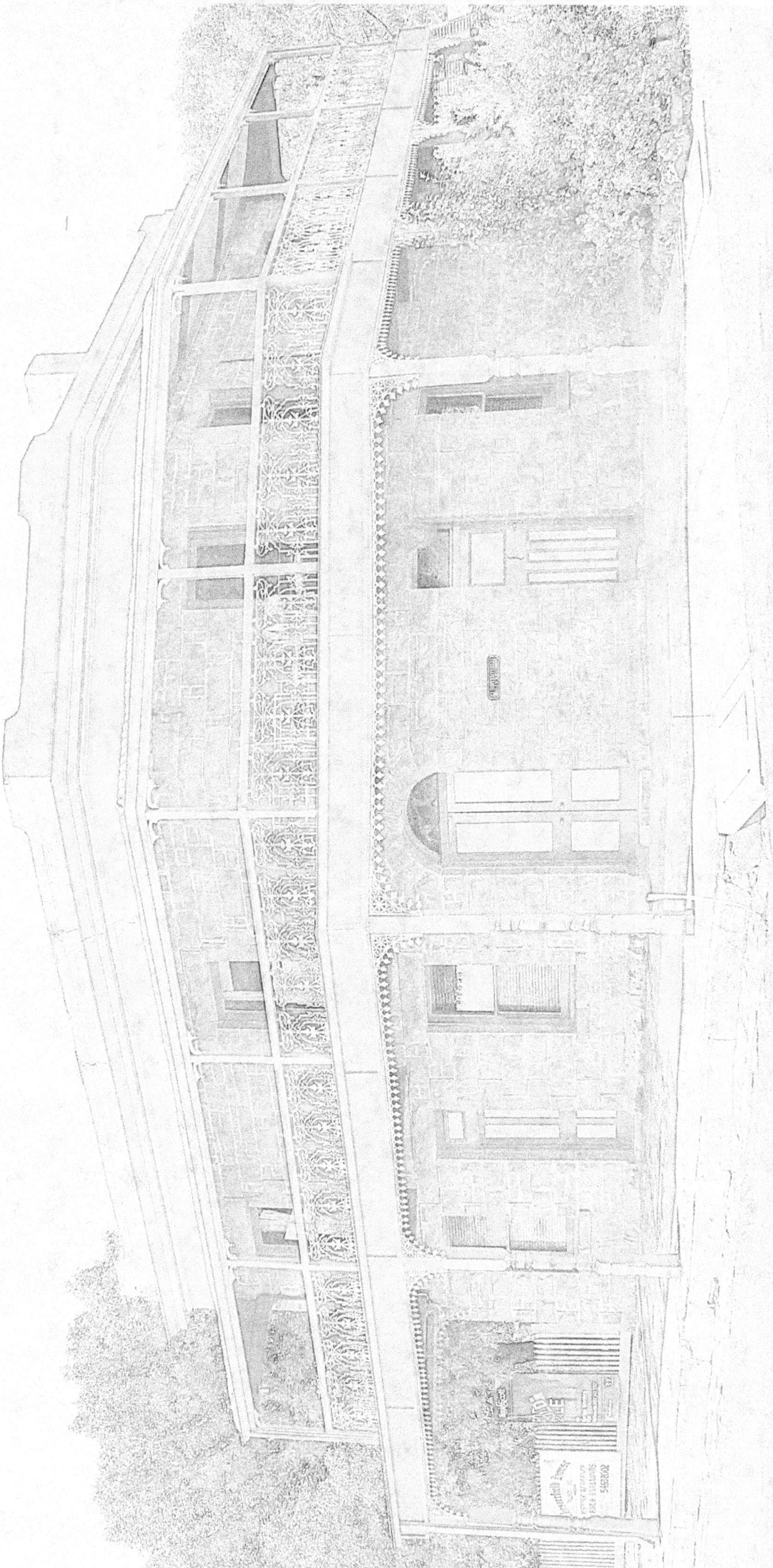

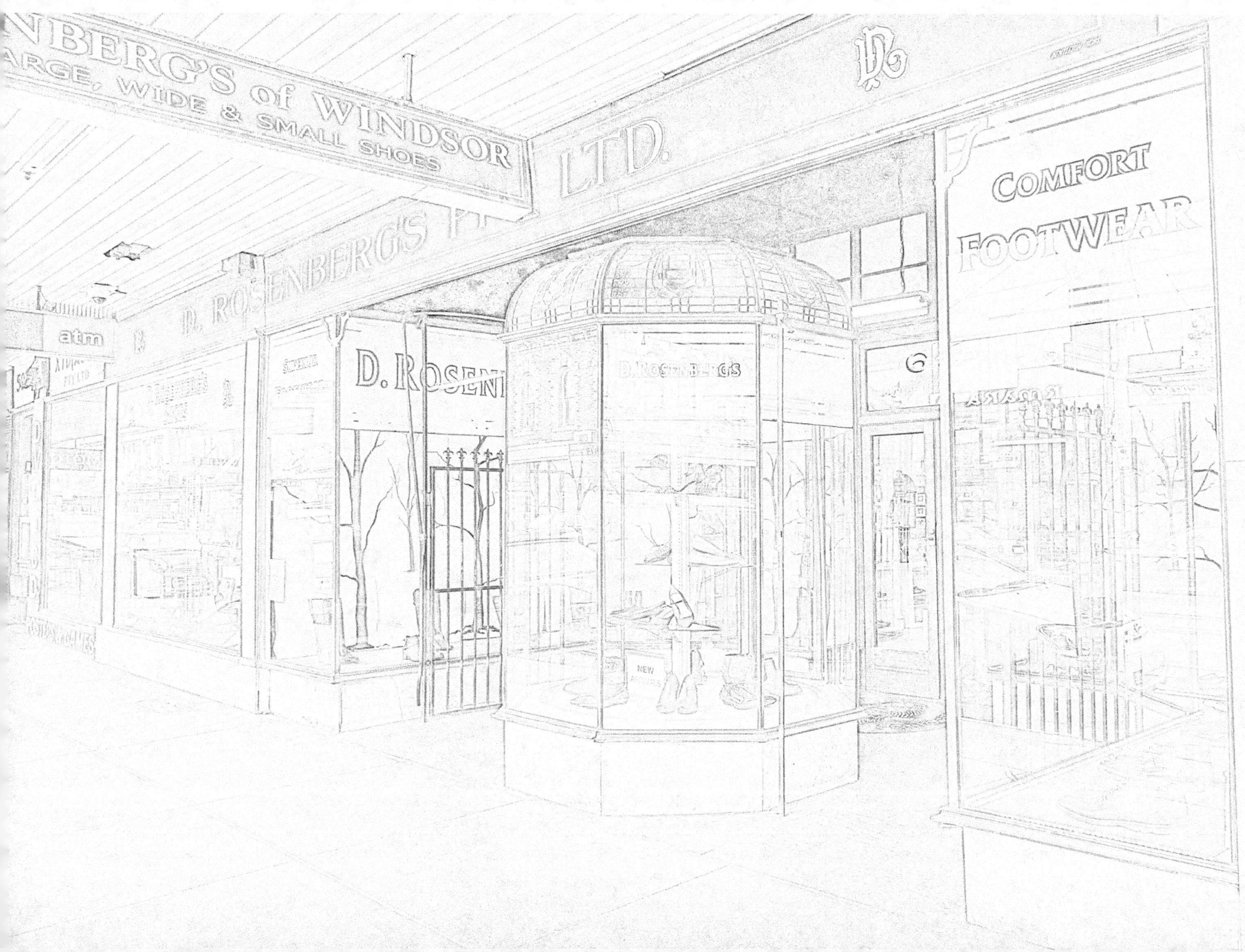
NBERG'S of WINDSOR
ARGE, WIDE & SMALL SHOES
LTD.
D. ROSENBERG'S
atm
D. ROSENI
D. ROSENBERGS
COMFORT
FOOTWEAR
NEW

www.ingramcontent.com/pod-product-compliance
Lightning Source LLC
Chambersburg PA
CBHW081056180526
45170CB00005B/1778
* 9 7 8 0 3 5 9 8 6 3 1 8 1 *